# Principles and Practices in Interscholastic Athletics: Guidelines for Administrators

# Principles and Practices in Interscholastic Athletics: Guidelines for Administrators

**James H. Humphrey**

Nova Science Publishers, Inc().
*New York*

**Senior Editors:** Susan Boriotti and Donna Dennis
**Coordinating Editor:** Tatiana Shohov
**Office Manager:** Annette Hellinger
**Graphics:** Wanda Serrano
**Book Production:** Matthew Kozlowski, Jonathan Rose and Jennifer Vogt
**Circulation:** Cathy DeGregory, Ave Maria Gonzalez, Raheem Miller and Andre Tillman
**Communications and Acquisitions:** Serge P. Shohov

*Library of Congress Cataloging-in-Publication Data*

Humphrey, James Harry, 1911-
    Principles and practices in interscholastic athletics: guidelines for administrators / James H. Humphrey.
        p. cm.
    Includes bibliographical references and index.
    ISBN 1-59033-159-1.
    1. School sports—United States—Management. 2. Sports administration—United States. I. Title.

GV346 .H86 2002
796'.06'0973—dc21

                                                                         2001059041

Copyright © 2002 by Nova Science Publishers, Inc.
                227 Main Street, Suite 100
                Huntington, New York 11743
                Tele. 631-424-NOVA (6682)        Fax 631-425-5933
                E Mail: Novascience@earthlink.net

All rights reserved. No part of this book may be reproduced, stored in a retrieval system or transmitted in any form or by any means: electronic, electrostatic, magnetic, tape, mechanical photocopying, recording or otherwise without permission from the publishers.

The authors and publisher have taken care in preparation of this book, but make no expressed or implied warranty of any kind and assume no responsibility for any errors or omissions. No liability is assumed for incidental or consequential damages in connection with or arising out of information contained in this book.

This publication is designed to provide accurate and authoritative information with regard to the subject matter covered herein. It is sold with the clear understanding that the publisher is not engaged in rendering legal or any other professional services. If legal or any other expert assistance is required, the services of a competent person should be sought. FROM A DECLARATION OF PARTICIPANTS JOINTLY ADOPTED BY A COMMITTEE OF THE AMERICAN BAR ASSOCIATION AND A COMMITTEE OF PUBLISHERS.

*Printed in the United States of America*

# ABOUT THE AUTHOR

James H. Humphrey, Professor Emeritus at the University of Maryland began his long and distinguished career as a public school director of physical education and athletics. Over the years he has authored or coauthored more than 50 books and edited more than 40 others. His articles and research reports have appeared in more than 20 different national and international journals and magazines. The recipient of numerous educational honors and awards, Dr. Humphrey is listed in the *International Authors and Writers whose Who and Contemporary Authors of Meritorious Works.*

# CONTENTS

List of Figures ..................................................................................... ix

Acknowledgments ............................................................................. xi

Preface ............................................................................................... xiii

Chapter 1: A Century of Interscholastic Athletics ........................... 1

Chapter 2: Philosophy and Objectives of Interscholastic Athletics ......... 13

Chapter 3: Functions of the Athletic Director ................................ 33

Chapter 4: Leadership in Interscholastic Athletics ........................ 53

Chapter 5: Organization and Administration of
    Interscholastic Athletics ................................................................ 65

Chapter 6: Scheduling for Athletic Competition ............................ 83

Chapter 7: Public Relations in Interscholastic Athletics ................ 97

Chapter 8: Athletic Directors Under Stress .................................... 107

Suggestions for Further Reading ...................................................... 127

Index .................................................................................................. 129

# LIST OF FIGURES

| | | |
|---|---|---|
| **Figure 1.** | Schematic Diagram of the Total Personality | 17 |
| **Figure 2.** | NIAAA Athletic Administrator Code of Ethics | 60 |
| **Figure 3.** | NFICA Coaches Code of Ethics | 63 |
| **Figure 4.** | State of Maryland Organization Chart | 67 |
| **Figure 5.** | Certificate for Care and Prevention of Athletic Injuries for Washington County, Maryland | 73 |
| **Figure 6.** | Single Elimination Tournament for Eight Teams | 84 |
| **Figure 7.** | Single Elimination Tournament for Six Teams | 86 |
| **Figure 8.** | Consolation Tournament for Eight Teams | 88 |
| **Figure 9.** | Consolation Tournament for Seven Teams | 89 |
| **Figure 10.** | Double Elimination Tournament for Eight Teams | 90 |
| **Figure 11.** | Double Elimination Tournament for Six Teams | 92 |
| **Figure 12.** | Procedure for Placement of Teams in Leagues | 93 |

# ACKNOWLEDGMENTS

A book is seldom the sole product of the author. Granted, the author does most of the things concerned with actually putting a book together, from the germ of the idea to seeing it through to final publication. It is almost always true, however, that many individuals participate, at least indirectly, in some way before a book is finally completed. This volume is no exception. I want to express my sincere appreciation to the hundreds of secondary school athletic directors who willingly gave of their time to participate in my extensive surveys. This source has been extremely valuable in providing relevant and compelling data for the book and I would like to thank them collectively.

There are certain individuals who can be singled out for special recognition for having made significant contributions to the book. They are: Robert A. Lombardi, Associate Executive Director of the Pennsylvania Interscholastic Athletic Association, Frank Kovaleski and Fritz McGinness, Assistant Executive Director and Associate Executive Director respectively of the National Federation of State High School Associations, Mary Etta Reedy, President, Maryland Public Secondary Schools Athletic Association, and John Tarman, Director of Marketing, California Interscholastic Federation.

Finally, I owe a debt of gratitude of the following secondary school athletic directors for providing important input that was an essential part of the book. Doug Douval, Mundelein, Illinois, Doug Grutchfield, Fitchburg, Massachusetts, Eugene Martin, Washigton County, Maryland, Mark Schlenoff, Baltimore, Maryland Polytechnic Institute, and Bill Sissel, Hoffman Estates, Illinois.

# PREFACE

Having started my career as a public school director of physical education and athletics, I still retain strong positive feelings about interscholastic athletics as a worthwhile aspect of the school program.

The inspiration to write this book was stimulated by several interviews with a number of secondary school athletic directors. This experience convinced me of the need for materials that are presented here.

In order to obtain a practical database for the book, I conducted some extensive surveys of several hundred secondary school athletic directors. Responses were received from directors in 42 states from communities ranging from less than ten thousand to more than a million in population. The study included a job analysis of secondary school athletic directors in which they were asked to rate more than 60 duties for frequency, difficulty, and importance. These data are woven throughout the text of the book as appropriate.

To my knowledge, data in this particular form are not available from any other source, which, of course, makes this book somewhat unique in its approach.

The initial chapter gives a brief overview of the history of interscholastic athletics with emphasis on interscholastics for girls and children of elementary school age.

Chapter 2 identifies and discusses physical, social, emotional, and intellectual objectives of athletics as they apply to the secondary school level.

In Chapter 3 a detailed account is given of the extensive job analysis study of secondary school athletic directors.

The fourth chapter deals with leadership in interscholastics at the state and local community levels.

Chapter 5 goes into some detail with regard to certain administrative practices and procedures, especially those identified by participants in my study.

Scheduling for competition is the subject of Chapter 6 and makes reference to the development of several different types of tournaments used in interscholastic athletic competition.

Public relations is discussed in Chapter 7 with special reference to the various agents and media that are important to the success of an interscholastic athletic program.

The final chapter considers the stressfulness of the secondary school athletic director's job. Various aspects of stress are discussed including its causes and methods of coping with it.

*Chapter 1*

# A CENTURY OF INTERSCHOLASTIC ATHLETICS

Although it is difficult to identify the exact date of the first interscholastic athletic contest, some historians[1] suggest that some private and public secondary schools were playing football as early as the 1880's. This same source has indicated that in the 1890s several city and county athletic associations were founded, such as the Cook County High School Association in the Chicago area.

These city and county associations evolved into district and state associations and in the early part of the $20^{th}$ century the state of Indiana founded a highly organized high school athletic association. A few years later Indiana University conducted a basketball tournament to determine a state high school champion.

In the early 1920s the National Federation of State High School Athletic Association was established to care for problems arising from interstate contests.

Since this auspicious beginning, interscholastic athletics have flourished on a large scale, particularly at the high school level.

At the present time in a majority of cases interscholastic athletics are structured so that local school athletic programs may look to state athletic or

---

[1] Rice, Emmett A, *A Brief History of Physical Education*, New York, A. S. Barnes and Company, 1929, p. 236-37.

activity associations for guidance in regulating the control of interscholastic athletics.

Most states devise rules and regulations for the protection of athletes in the member schools. This is accomplished in part by such procedures as limiting the number of contests, providing state insurance and benefit plans, and approving athletic officials.

## INTERSCHOLASTIC ATHLETICS FOR GIRLS

For the most part, over the years the major focus of interscholastic athletics has been on the boys' programs. However, there has been a slow but gradual change in this regard.

In the early days of interscholastic athletics many educators frowned upon participation for girls. Rampant complaints centered around such factors as the "weaker sex" and "unladylike practices." There was particular reference to the notion that such participation was too strenuous for the female sex. To compensate in part for this type of thinking the game of basketball for females through the 1920s had six girls completing a team. Three were on offense and three were on defense. The offense played on one half of the court and the defense played on the other half. The theory was that such a plan would be only half as strenuous for girls. However, it was not too long before this system was revised to comply with "boys' rules." Incidentally, at the present time girls' interscholastic basketball is very popular in some communities.

Of particular importance to girls' interscholastic athletics over the years has been the National Association for Girls and Women in Sports, which celebrated its 100$^{th}$ anniversary in 1999. This is a nonprofit organization designed to serve the needs of administrators, teachers, coaches, officials, leaders, media, and participants, of sports programs for girls and women.[2]

Another important milestone for girls' interscholastic athletics was the passage of the federal law known as Title IX of the Educational Amendments of 1972 designed to end sex discrimination in American education. A factor to keep in mind is that compliance with Title IX means *equal opportunity* and not *equal programs*. Under this action all students- boys and girls alike -

---

[2] Griffin Joy, NAGWS Centenial: Celebrating the past, shaping the future, *Journal of Physical Education*, Recreation, and Dance, April 1999, p. 17.

should benefit from the potential values that interscholastic athletics have to offer.

In recent years an interesting phenomenon had developed. This has to do with girls participating on boys' teams and vice versa. In fact, there have been some isolated cases where girls have excelled over boys in such sports as wrestling. On the reverse side, some boys have felt that they are entitled to participate in field hockey – traditionally considered to be a sport only for girls. However, in recent years where boys have petitioned school systems to allow them to play field hockey, they have lost more cases than they have won.[3]

This raises the whole question of gender differences, with particular reference to physical activity. This is perhaps worthy of the following detailed discussion on this subject, especially since it is a problem that school personnel is increasingly having to deal with.

## Gender Differences

Of course, there are structural (anatomical) and functional (physiological) differences; however, because these differences are so well known, reference will be made only to them in terms of the differences in some of the basic physical skill performances between males and females.

The basic locomotor skill of *running* there is little difference in performance of boys and girls of elementary school age. However, after that time boys increase their speed and endurance over girls. Although this may be true on the average, many girls become excellent performers in distance running. For example, just a few years ago it would have been outside the realm of logical thought that women would be capable of engaging in Marathon running. Nonetheless, in modern times, world class female Marathoners regularly are timed in what would have been credible performance for males a few decades ago.

In the skill of *jumping* there are many varieties in performance of children. Generally speaking, they tend to improve their performance as they get older and improvement tends to be more pronounced for boys than girls.

---

[3] Robbins, Alexandra, Boys on girls' teams stir controversy, *USA Today,* March 16, 1999.

In the propulsion skills, especially *throwing,* gender differences in the early behavior of children in this skill is substantially favorable for boys. At all age levels, boys are generally superior to girls in throwing for distance, although there is not as much a pronounced gender difference in throwing for accuracy.

In order to have a more complete understanding of the whole area of gender differences we need to start at birth. When entering the world, the male child comes in with some degree of fanfare- "IT'S A BOY!!" The female more often than not is likely to get a more suppressed announcement – "You have a little girl." Expectations are likely to be muck loftier for males – "Maybe he will grow up to be president." Not often a greeting for baby girls.

Interestingly enough, immediately after they are born we seem to relegate girls to somewhere between second and third class citizenship by dressing them in *pink* and boys in *blue*. If the reader will indulge me while I delve into the field of color psychology with a bit of wild speculation, perhaps I can explain. As we know, in certain kinds of competition first place is designated by a blue ribbon, second place, by a red ribbon, and third place, by a white ribbon. Thus, do we automatically declare boy babies winners over girl babies at the outset by garbing them in blue and by placing girls somewhere between second and third place – pink being a combination of red and white?

In any case, from a growth and developmental point of view, while at birth the female is from one-half to one centimeter less in length than the male and around 300 grams less in weight, she is actually a much better developed organism. It is estimated on the average that at the time of entrance into school, the female is usually 6 to 12 months more physically mature than the male. As a result, girls tend to learn earlier how to perform such task of manual dexterity as buttoning their clothing. In one of my own observational studies of preschool children some years ago, it was found that little girls were able to perform the task of tying their shoelaces at a rate of almost four times that of little boys.

Due to certain hormonal conditions, boys tend to be more aggressive, restless, and impatient. In addition, the male has more rugged bone and muscular structure, and, as a consequence, greater strength than that of females at all ages. Because of this, males tend to display greater muscular reactivity which in turn expresses itself in a stronger tendency toward restlessness and vigorous activity. This condition is concerned with the greater oxygen consumption required to fulfill the male's need for increased energy production. The male organism might be compared to an engine which operates at higher levels of speed and intensity than the less energetic female organism. Over three decades ago in a conversation with the late Dr. Franklin Henry of the University of California, he informed me that he had found in his research that males have what might be termed an "active response set" whereas females might have a "reactive response set." This could be interpreted to mean that males confront the environment with an activity orientation while females have a response orientation.

Another factor to be taken into account is the difference in Basal Metabolic Rate (BMR) in young boys and girls. The BMR is indicative of the speed at which body fuel is changed into energy, as well as how fast this energy is used. BMR can be measured in terms of calories per meter of body surface with a calorie representing a unit measure of heat energy in food. It has been found that on average BMR rises from birth to about three years of age and then starts to decline until the ages of 20 to 24. The BMR is higher for boys than for girls. Because of the higher BMR, boys will in turn have a higher amount of energy to expend. Because of differences in sex hormonal conditions and BMR, it appears logical to assume that these factors will influence the male in his behavior patterns.

Some studies have shown that as far as hyperactivity and attention deficit disorder is concerned, boys may outnumber girls by a ratio as much as 9 to 1. This may be the reason why teachers generally tend to rate young males as being so much more aggressive than females with the result that young boys are considered to be more negativistic and extraverted. Because of these characteristics, boys generally have poorer relationships with their teachers than do girls, and in terms of behavior problems and discipline in the age range from five to nine, boys account for twice as many disturbances as girls. The importance of this factor is borne out when it is considered that good teacher-pupil relationships tend to raise the achievement levels of both sexes.

Various studies have shown that girls generally receive higher grades than boys despite the fact that boys may achieve as well, and in some instances, better than girls. It is also clearly evident that boys in the early years fail twice as often as girls even when there is no significant differences between intelligence and achievement test scores of both sexes. This suggests that even though both sexes have the same intellectual tools, there are other factors that militate against learning as far as boys are concerned.

Although all of his may be true for preteen boys, the situation seems to change for girls after about 13 years of age. After that time many aspects of society become anxiety-provoking for girls. This may be especially true of the school environment. Research in recent years on this subject has revealed some interesting results, some of which can be summarized as follows.

1. There is little encouragement for girls to pursue mathematics and science.
2. There are subtle teacher practices, such as calling on boys more often or gearing school activities more to the males.
3. Boys call out answers eight times more often than girls. When boys call out, teachers are more apt to listen.
4. When boys do not answer, teachers seem more likely to encourage them to give answers or opinions than they are to encourage girls.
5. Girls are at a disadvantage in taking tests because such tests may be geared to male performance. Taking this into account, some standard intelligence tests now have a masculinity-feminity index.
6. Although there does not appear to be much difference in test anxiety between girls and boys, at the same time girls are prone to suffer more stress over report cards than do boys.
7. Teachers appear to encourage male students to work with laboratory equipment, especially in the more complex sciences.
8. Vocational education programs are often geared to boys in spite of the fact that a large percentage of the work force is female.
9. Stereotypical images still appear in textbooks, with an overwhelming number of male authors and role models studied in the class.

Some school systems are attempting to correct some of these conditions by inaugurating *gender equity* programs. What really needs to be taken into account is the emotional stress that is place on both of the sexes, particularly girls.

As we know, the condition of *stress* is a highly individualized, subjective perception. Nevertheless, one expert on the subject, Helen Kearney[4] once raised the question: "Is there a commonality of stressors to which women are uniquely susceptible?" To this, the consensus is affirmative, as is the judgment that such stressors have multiplied at a rate far in excess of those of their male counterparts. This is attributed in large measure to radical changes in societal norms which have attended women's suffrage, the feminist movement, dramatic rates of divorce, increased geographical mobility, discontinuity is extended family relationships, and a steady influx of women into occupations and professions, previously the proprietary interest of males.

So much for gender differences. Obviously, the reader will draw his or her own conclusions with regard to the preceding detailed discussion.

## ELEMENTARY SCHOOL INTERSCHOLASTIC ATHLETICS

Although certain aspects of secondary school interscholastic athletics have been faulted at various times, by far the greatest amount of controversy has been concerned with the elementary school level.

Athletic competition between elementary schools got its start very early in the 20th century when the Public Schools Athletic League in New York City was organized. The purpose of the League was to encourage and manage athletic contests among elementary schools, and to direct the so-called competitive spirit in a way most beneficial to children. The idea caught on rapidly and many large cities adopted the plan.

Over the years there have been strong proponents as well as equally forceful opponents of the practice. Two of the main reasons why many educators and child development specialists oppose elementary school interscholastic athletics are (1) the effect of *competition* on young children and (2) the possibility of serious *injuries*. Let us examine the premise.

---

[4] Kearney, Helen McCready, Female stress: An overview, *Practical Stress Management, The Newsletter of the American Institute of Stress,* May/June 1985.

## Competition as a Factor in Children's Athletic Activities

The positive and negative aspects of athletic competition for children has been debated for decades. In fact, over 40 years ago I was the chairman of a national committee of "Competition for Children." After studying the matter with some degree of thoroughness, the only conclusion that the "experts" on our committee could come up with was that the success or failure of such competition was dependent upon the type of supervision provided for overseeing such programs.

There has always been a concern for the emotional stress that competition can have on a child. And, of course, such emotional stress can impact on a child's physical well-being.

In a study conducted with 200 fifth and sixth grade children, one of the questions I asked was "What is the one thing that *worries* you most in school?" As might be expected there were a variety of responses. However, the one general characteristic that tended to emerge was the emphasis placed on competition in so many school situations. Although students did not state this specifically, the nature of their responses clearly seemed to be along these lines.

Most of the literature on competition for children has focused on sports activities; however, there are many situations that exist in some classrooms that can cause competitive stress. An example is that antiquated "Spelling Bee" which still exists in some schools, and in fact, continues to be recognized in an annual national competition. Perhaps the first few children "spelled down" are likely to be the ones who need spelling practice the most. And, to say the least, it can be embarrassing in front of others to fail in any school task.

It is interesting to note that the terms *cooperation* and *competition* are antonymous; therefore, the reconciliation of children's competitive needs and cooperative needs is not an easy matter. In a sense we are confronted with an ambivalent condition which, if not carefully handled, could place children in a state of conflict, thus causing them to suffer distress.

This was recognized by Karen Horney[5] well over half a century ago when she indicted that we must not only be assertive but aggressive, able to push

---

[5] Horney, Karen, *The Neurotic Personality of Our Times,* New York, W. W. Norton and Company, Inc., 1937, p. 116.

others out of the way. On the other hand, we are deeply imbued with ideals which declare that it is selfish to want anything for ourselves, that we should be humble, turn the other hand, be yielding. Thus, society not only rewards one kind of behavior (cooperation) but its direct opposite (competition). Perhaps more often than not our cultural demands sanction these rewards without provision of clear-cut standards of value with regard to specific conditions under which these forms of behavior might well be practiced. Thus, the child is placed in somewhat of a quandary as to when to compete and when to cooperate.

More recently it has been found that competition does not necessarily lead to peak performance, and may in fact interfere with achievement. In this connection, Kohn[6] reported on a survey on the effects of competition in sports, business and classroom achievement and found that 65 studies showed that cooperation promoted higher achievement than competition, eight showed the reverse and 36 showed no statistically significant differences. It was concluded that he trouble with competition is that it makes one person's success depend upon another's failure, and as a result when success depends upon sharing resources, competition can get in the way.

In generalizing on the basis of the available evidence with regard to the subject of competition it seems justifiable to formulate the following concepts:

1. Very young children in general are not very competitive but become more so as they grow older.
2. There is a wide variety in competition among children; that is, some are violently competitive, while others are mildly competitive, and still others are not competitive at all.
3. Boys are more competitive than girls.
4. Competition should be adjusted so that there is not a preponderant number of winners over losers.
5. Competition and rivalry can sometimes produce results in effort and speed of accomplishment.
6. Adults involved in children's athletics might well be guided by the above concepts.

---

[6] Kohn, A. *No Contest: The Case Against Competition,* Boston, Houghton-Mifflin, 1986, p. 142.

Whether one is a proponent or critic of competitive athletics for children it has not become evident that such competition may be "here to stay," at least as far as *out-of-school* programs are concerned. Thus, controlling such programs might be our greatest problem. This might perhaps be done by concentrating our efforts in the direction of educating both adults and children regarding the positive and negative effects of competition.

**Injuries as a Factor in Children's Athletic Activities**

The thing that concerns parents, particularly mothers, most about their children's participation in athletics is the possibility of injury. It should be borne in mind that contrary to popular opinion, accidents resulting in injury do not "just happen." On the other hand, over 90 percent of such accidents are caused. Although injuries do occur, many of them can be avoided if proper precautions are taken.

There are certain conditions traditionally associated with athletics. "Tennis elbow" is a case in point. This is an inflammation of the rounded portion of the bone at the elbow joint. The name is no doubt a misnomer because the majority of cases are a result of activities other than swinging a tennis racquet.

The same could probably be said of what has become commonly known as "Little League elbow." The technical name for this condition is *osteochondritis capitulum* which like "tennis elbow" is an inflammation of a bone and its cartilage at the elbow joint. It is caused generally by a hard and prolonged act of throwing using the overarm throwing pattern. One would not have to be a "Little Leaguer" to contract this condition. Simply playing catch and throwing hard to a partner for prolonged periods could also bring this about.

One of the most feared injuries in athletics, or any activity for that matter, are those to the eyes. In this regard Orlando[7] did an interesting study to determine the severity and frequency of soccer-related eye injuries. The medical charts of 13 soccer players who had sustained blunt trauma to the eye were reviewed. The patients (five girls and eight boys) ranged in age from 8 to

---

[7] Orlando, R. G., Soccer-related eye injuries in children and adolescents, *Physician and Sports Medicine,* November 1988, p. 7.

15 years. The most common injury was *hyphemia* (a hemorrhage in the eyeball). Others included *retinal edema* (excessive accumulation of fluid in the innermost layer of the eye), *secondary glaucoma* (increased pressure within the eyeball), *chorioretinal rupture* (an inflammatory condition in the back of the eye), and *angle recession.* Six injuries were caused by the soccer ball, three by a kick, and one by a head butt. In three cases the cause was unknown. As a result of the study, the author made the following recommendations: (1) education of coaching staff, parents and officials; (2) protective eye wear; (3) proper conditioning; (4) strictly enforced rules, and (5) an emphasis on having fun to help reduce the number and severity of soccer related eye injuries.

For over 40 years some critics have been concerned with possible injuries that children might sustain in *contact* sports, especially football. This concern has centered around the notion that too much pressure would be applied to the *epiphyses*, particular in such activities as football.

In the long bones there is first a center of ossification for the bone called the *diaphysis* and one or more centers for each extremity called the *epiphyses.* Ossification proceeds from the diaphysis toward the epiphysis, and from the epiphysis toward the diaphysis. As each new portion is ossified thin layers of cartilage continue to develop between the diaphysis and epiphysis and during this period of growth, these outstrip ossification. When this ceases the growth of the bone stops. Injury can occur as a result of trauma which could be due to a "blow" incurred in a contact sport.

If we are to be successful in our efforts to avoid injuries to child sports participants, more emphasis needs to be exerted in the direction of preventive measures. Such measures can be taken by those persons who have direct responsibility of working with children in sports activities – particularly those activities that do not come under the jurisdiction of the school.

As mentioned previously, and in general, educators do not recommend that highly competitive interscholastic athletics be included in the elementary school. In the absence of solid scientific evidence regarding the effect of highly competitive forms of athletic activity upon children of elementary school age, it seems important that subjective opinion of leaders in the field of physical education and child development serve as guiding criteria to determine whether or not interscholastic athletic activities should be included as an elementary school extra class activity. At the present the preponderance of such opinion appears to indicate that highly competitive interscholastic athletics should be excluded from the elementary school program.

In the final analysis, the positive or negative influence that highly competitive activities will have on elementary school children will no doubt be governed by the extent and type of supervision provided for such programs. This is to say that it is possible to have this type of program and that it can possibly meet the needs of some children with superior ability. However, the emphasis should be placed on fun and enjoyment rather than on winning.

In summarizing this initial chapter, there seems to be little question that the whole area of interscholastic athletics has traveled an interesting and sometimes uncertain path during the last 100 years. As we move into the 21$^{st}$ century it is difficult to predict the future of this area of the school program. In any case, however, as long as the welfare of the participants is not compromised, there is perhaps no limit to the positive potential of this experience as an important educational endeavor.

*Chapter 2*

# PHILOSOPHY AND OBJECTIVES OF INTERSCHOLASTIC ATHLETICS

Whether they are aware of it or not, all individuals have developed some sort of philosophy of life. They may not have put it into so many words, but their philosophy is manifested in their daily actions. Regardless of the professional endeavor in which one chooses to engage, he or she will have some sort of philosophy about it. Thus, those persons who are involved in interscholastic athletics maintain a philosophy about the field. The development of such a philosophy should begin soon after one begins to prepare for a career in athletics. One's philosophy need not necessarily remain static and may be subject to change as the needs of society change.

In line with developing a philosophy one needs to give very serious consideration to the objectives of interscholastic athletics. This is to say that is necessary to have an understanding of the potential contributions athletics can make to participants and to proceed in a manner whereby these contributions might be realized.

## MEANING OF TERMS

A standard dictionary definition of the term *philosophy* usually refers to it as a pursuit of wisdom or enlightenment. Another generalized description of the term is that it concerns our fundamental beliefs or practicing those things in which we believe. More specifically, a philosophy of interscholastic athletics is concerned with a careful systematic intellectual endeavor in which we attempt to see athletics as a whole and at the same time as an integral part of the culture of man.

The term *objective* appears to have been adopted by education from the military. The latter uses it to identify an area to be assaulted and/or captured in some way. The *Dictionary of Education* gives the following definition of the term: "Aim, end in view, or purpose of a course of action or a belief; that which is anticipated as desirable in the early phases of an activity and serves to select, regulate, and direct later aspects of the activity so that the total process is designed and integrated."[1]

It is noted that various other terms are used to convey the same meaning. Some of these include *aim, goal,* and *purpose.* Regardless of the particular term used, we might well consider it with regard to a very simple meaning; that is, where are we trying to go or what are we trying to accomplish through the medium of interscholastic athletics?

## DEVELOPING A PHILOSOPHY AND FORMULATING OBJECTIVES

Until about the twelfth century, few European sailors were willing to sail far beyond the sight of land because on the open seas they had no reliable way of knowing whether they were on course or not. Then the compass became known in Europe. From that time on seamen had something to sail by and thus could travel in all kinds of weather with considerable confidence that they were moving in the direction they wished. The compass made possible the explorations of such people as Columbus and Magellan, who first sailed around the world.

Those in the field of interscholastic athletics also need something to guide their efforts, a guiding philosophy so to speak. Otherwise they are like sailors of long ago who sailed about aimlessly when away from land, now moving this way, that way – but without any real confidence that they are "on course" and moving as they should. At times they need to be able to "check the course" by referring to a compass in their own minds so as to know if they are moving in the proper direction. In order to do this they must have a magnetic

---

[1] Good, Carter V., *Dictionary of Education*, New York, McGraw-Hill, 1959, p. 371.

north composed of clearly defined, desirable, and worthwhile objectives. If they have their objectives in mind as they make decisions about their programs, they will not be sailing blind. If they do not, they will have no basis for knowing whether or not they are doing the right thing and making wise decisions.

This problem of philosophy and objectives applies to living in general. Many people are unhappy and feel their lives are empty simply because they have never thought out for themselves what is important to them and what they really wish to achieve in life. Without a philosophy to guide their thinking and actions they are like sea voyagers without a compass so of course they feel lost. Similarly, in those situations where athletic experiences are not very effective, there is a very good chance that the people in charge of it are confused about the purpose of their work and are failing to operate in terms of desirable and worthwhile objectives.

Above all, objectives should always be in the best interest of the individual. This precludes the practice of some coaches using an injured player simply because their philosophy is concerned only with winning.

The approach taken here is that athletics should be looked upon as a means of providing experiences which benefit the *whole* person; that is, athletics has objectives which apply to the *total personality* of those who participate in them.

## THE CONCEPT OF TOTAL PERSONALITY DEVELOPMENT

A great deal of clinical and experimental evidence indicates that a human being must be considered as a whole and not a collection of parts. Some terms used to describe this situation are "whole child," "unified individual," and "total personality." The latter term is commonly used in the fields of mental health and psychology and is gaining more usage in the field of education. Moreover, when we consider it from a point of view of one existing as a person, it is interesting to note that "existence as a person" is one rather common definition of personality.

What then comprises the total personality? Anyone who had difficulty in formulating views with regard to what the human personality actually consists of can take courage in the knowledge that many experts who spend their time studying it are not always in complete agreement as to what it is or how it operates. Indeed, one of the greatest mysteries which confronts man in modern society is man himself. If one were to analyze the literature on the subject it would be found generally that the total personality consists of the sum of all the *physical, social, emotional* and *intellectual* aspects of any individual. The total personality is *one* thing comprising these various major aspects. All of these components are highly interrelated and interdependent. All are of importance to the balance and health of the personality because only in terms of their health can the personality as a whole maintain a completely healthy state. The condition of any one aspect affects each other aspect to a degree and hence the personality as a whole.

When a nervous person stutters or becomes nauseated, a mental state is *not* causing a physical symptom. On the contrary, a pressure imposed upon the organism causes a series of reactions which include thought, verbalization, digestive processes, and muscular function. Mind does not cause the body to become upset; the *total* organism is upset by a situation and reflects its upset in several ways, including disturbance in thought, feeling, and bodily processes. The whole individual responds in interaction with the social and physical environment. As the individual is affected by the environment, he or she in turn has an effect upon it.

However, because of a long tradition during which physical development *or* intellectual development, rather than physical *and* intellectual, has been glorified, we often times are still accustomed to dividing the two in our thinking. The result may be that we sometimes pull human beings apart with this kind of thinking.

Traditional attitudes which separate mind and body tend to lead to unbalanced development of an individual with respect to mind and body and/or social adjustment. To understand better the concept of total personality the human organism can be seen in terms of the diagram in Figure 1.

The circle is the total environment of the individual which circumscribes and confines all aspects of the total personality. The triangle with its three sides – physical, emotional, and intellectual aspects of the total personality – form a single figure with the *physical* aspect as a base. An arrow, extending from the center of the triangle upward through one of the sides, is designated *social* to represent interpersonal relationships within the field of the individual and the environment. The arrow is pointed at both ends to suggest a two-way process; the individual is affected by those around him, and he in turn has some effect upon them. The triangle is dependent upon a balance of all its parts, and if one part of the triangle is changed, the entire triangle is reshaped. It is interesting to draw diagrams in which one after the other of the sides is shortened – as in one kind or another of developmental failure or retardation – and see how this affects the triangle. It is also interesting to make personal application such as the following: What happens to my intellectual performance when I am worried or have a stomachache? What changes occur in my body when I feel frightened, embarrassed, or angered?

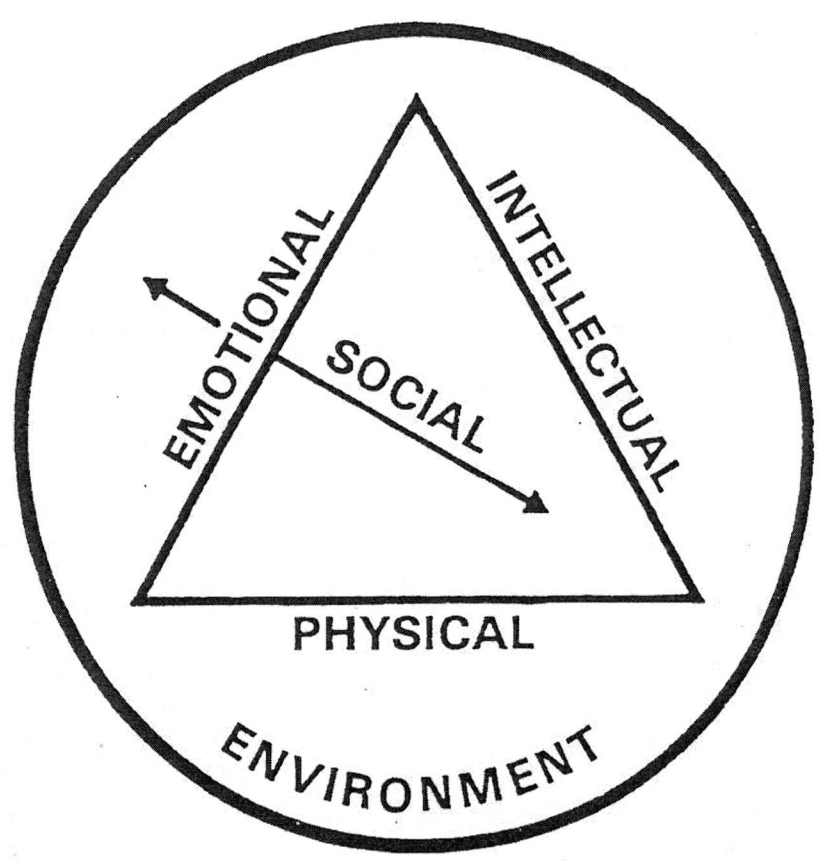

**Figure 1.** Schematic Diagram of the Total Personality

It is interesting that in modern times, when great emphasis is placed on social adjustment, that perhaps a major problem involves faulty interpersonal relationships. For this reason it is important to make special note of the interaction between the individual and the environment. The quality of the individual's interpersonal relationships affects all the other aspects of his or her personality. How well can you concentrate when you think someone is talking about you? These are social circumstances which affect the physical, emotional, and intellectual aspects of personality.

This matter of interpersonal relationships is still more fundamental to development of individuals than the foregoing illustration suggests. It has been found that infants and very young children who are deprived of a reasonable amount of mothering – that initial and basic social experience – actually stop growing in one or more aspects of their total personality, even though all of their needs are met. Some fail to develop mentally; some show both physical immaturity and mental retardation. Still others are affected mainly at the emotional level; that is, if they are deprived of love and given instead non-loving care, they may fail to grow emotionally and not be capable of human feeling as we generally think of it. In brief, the quality of interpersonal relationships in the early years may tend to set the pattern of subsequent patterns attitudes and behavior toward other people, authority, and the "rules of the game" of life generally.

All of these things then are the basis of total personality – a complex balance of psychophysical and social considerations which prepare the individual for the fullest, most socially valuable, productive, and adventuresome living.

The foregoing statements have attempted to point out rather forcefully that the identified components of the total personality – physical, social, emotional, and intellectual – characterize the totality of being. The fact that each of these aspects warrants a separate discussion. This appears to be extremely important if one is to understand fully the place of each aspect as an integral part of the whole personality. The following discussions of the physical, social, emotional, and intellectual aspects of personality as they relate to interscholastic athletics should be viewed in this general frame of reference.

As these aspects of total personality are discussed, there will emerge objectives of interscholastic athletics as they relate to the various aspects. There will emerge a *physical objective* of athletics, a *social objective* of athletics, and *emotional objective* of athletics and an *intellectual objective* of athletics. The reason for this approach to the formulating of objectives of interscholastic athletics lies in the fact that in order to make a valid exploration of the area of athletics in the school program, it becomes necessary to consider the guiding philosophy and purpose of education as a whole. The necessity of this consideration becomes most important when one takes into account that the basic philosophy which guides the entire educational program should also apply to athletics.

If one were to analyze the various statements of purpose of the whole of education which have been made by responsible educational groups through the years, it would be a relatively easy matter to identify a constantly emerging pattern. These statements have gradually evolved into a more or less general agreement among present-day educational leaders that the general goal of education is to stimulate and guide the growth of an individual so that he or she will function in life activities involving vocation, citizenship, and enriched leisure; and further stimulate the individual so that he or she will possess as high a level of physical, social, emotional, and intellectual development as the individual capacity will permit. If it is a valid assumption that the purpose of education is to attempt to insure development of the total personality, then it is incumbent upon those in interscholastic athletics to explore these developmental processes as they relate to athletics.

In this regard a recent study by Yin and Ryska[2] is of interest. They attempted to determine the relationship between participation in interscholastic sports and various academic and psychological indices among middle and high school students. They found that self-esteem and average grade point average were significantly higher in student athletes than student non-athletes. In addition, the risk for school dropout rate was significantly lower for student athletes. The researchers concluded that these findings may provide new insight into the ongoing debate regarding the roles of school athletic programs as well as the relative impact of such programs on the secondary school student.

---

[2] Yin, Zenong and Ryska, Todd A., Reexamining the roles of interscholastic sports participation in education. *Research Quarterly for Exercise and Sports,* March 1999 Supplement, p. A 131.

## THE PHYSICAL ASPECT OF PERSONALITY

One point of departure in discussing the physical aspect of personality could be to state that "everybody has a body." Some are short, some are tall, some are lean, and some are fat. People come in different sizes but all of them have a certain innate capacity which is influenced by the environment.

As far as any individual is concerned, it might be said that he or she *is* his or her body. It is the base of operation – what was previously referred to as the "physical base." The other components of the total personality - social, emotional, and intellectual – are somewhat vague as far as some individuals are concerned. Although these are manifested in various ways, a person does not necessarily see them as he or she does the physical aspect. Consequently it becomes all important that one be helped early in life to gain control over the physical aspect, to develop what is known as basic body control. The ability to do this of course will vary from one person to another. It will depend upon the status of physical fitness of the individual. The broad area of physical fitness can be broken down into certain components, and it is important that individuals achieve to the best of their natural ability as far as these components, and it is important that individuals achieve to the best of their natural ability as far as these components are concerned. There is not complete agreement as far as identification of the components of physical fitness is concerned. However, the following information provided by the President's Council on Physical Fitness and Sports considers certain components to be basic as follows:

1. *Muscular strength.* This refers to the contraction power of the muscles. The strength of muscles is usually measured with dynamometers or tensiometers which record the amount of force particular muscle groups can apply in a single maximum effort. Man's existence and effectiveness depend upon the muscles. All movements of the body or any of its parts are impossible without action by muscles attached to the skeleton. Muscles perform vital functions of the body as well. The heart is a muscle; death occurs when it ceases to contract. Breathing, digestion, and elimination are impossible without muscular contractions. These vital muscular functions are influenced by exercising the skeletal muscles; the heart beats faster, the blood circulates through the

body at a greater rate, breathing comes deep and rapid, and perspiration breaks out on the surface of the skin.

2. *Muscular endurance.* Muscular endurance is the ability of muscles to perform work. Two variations of muscular endurance are recognized: *isometric* whereby a maximum static muscular contraction is held and *isotonic* whereby the muscles continue to raise and lower a sub-maximal load as in weight training or performing push-ups. In the isometric form, they alternately shorten and lengthen. Muscular endurance must assume some muscular strength. However, there are distinctions between the two; muscle groups of the same strength may possess different degrees of endurance.

3. *Circulatory-respiratory endurance.* Circulatory-respiratory endurance is characterized by moderate contractions of large muscle groups for relatively long periods of time during which maximal adjustments of the circulatory-respiratory system to the activity are necessary, as in distance running and swimming. Obviously, strong and enduring muscles are needed. However, by themselves they are not enough; they do not guarantee well-developed circulatory-respiratory functions.

In addition to the basic three above, there are other components of physical fitness to be considered:

*Muscular power.* Ability to release maximum muscular force in the shortest time. Example: standing long jump.

*Agility.* Speed in changing body positions or in changing direction. Example: dodging run.

*Speed.* Rapidity with which successive movements of the same kind can be performed. Example: 50-yard dash.

*Flexibility.* Range of movements in a joint or a sequence of joints. Example: touch fingers to floor without bending knees.

*Balance.* Ability to maintain position and equilibrium both in movement (dynamic balance) and while stationary (static balance). Examples: Walking on a line or balance beam (dynamic); standing on one foot (static).

*Coordination.* Working together of the muscles and organs of the human body in the performance of a specific task. Example: throwing or catching an object.

The components of physical fitness and hence the physical aspects of personality aspect of personality can be measured with calibrated instruments, as in the case of measuring muscle strength mentioned above. Moreover, we can tell how tall or how heavy one is at any stage development. We can derive others accurate data with measurements of blood pressure, blood counts, urinalysis, and the like.

## PHYSICAL OBJECTIVES

It may be generally stated that a good program of interscholastic athletics can be considered a stimulant to physical growth. Moreover, the general consensus indicates that participation in a well-balanced athletic program is an important way of maintaining optimum health.

Two major objectives emerge as far as the physical aspect of personality is concerned. The first of these takes into account *maintaining a suitable level of physical fitness.* Second, there is the consideration of the *development of skill and ability.*

### Maintaining a Suitable Level of Physical Fitness

Physical fitness presupposes an adequate intake of good food and an adequate amount of rest and sleep; but beyond these things activity involving all the big muscles of the body is essential. Just how high a level of physical fitness should be maintained from one state to another is difficult to determine because we must raise the question: "Fitness for what?" Obviously, the young varsity athlete needs to think of a level of fitness far above that which will concern the average middle-aged individual.

Physical fitness has been described in different ways by different people; however, when all of these descriptions are put together it is likely that they will be characterized more by their similarities than their differences. For purposes here I will think of physical fitness as the level of ability of the human organism to perform certain physical tasks or, put another way, the fitness to perform various specified tasks requiring muscular effort.

## Development of Skill and Ability

The second major physical objective of athletics has to do with disciplined body movement. The physically educated individual, commensurate with his or her capacity and within his or her own limitations, is adept in a variety of athletic activities. We enjoy those activities in which we are reasonably proficient. We are dealing with an important principle related to our athletic objectives; that is, if people are to enjoy participating in an activity, they need to be reasonably competent in the skills involved in the activity. Consequently, there must be objectives both in terms of the *number* of skills to which student athletes are introduced and the level of competence to be achieved so that they will associate a pleasurable experience with participation.

We must reckon with another matter that is closely related to competence in a wide variety of skills. Some physical education teachers have stressed the very strenuous team sports in their programs and others have placed emphasis on what have been called "life-time sports" which may be used later on in life. A sensible point of view on this subject would appear to be that we should develop competence in a variety of skills for use *now and in the future*. Stated more specifically, as an objective of athletics it could be said that all individuals should be prepared by their athletic experience to participate in suitable and satisfying activities for use now and in the future.

In summary, the physical object of athletic should imply organic development commensurate with vigor, vitality, strength, balance, flexibility, and neuromuscular coordination, together with the development of skill and ability in a variety of activities for use now and in the future.

## THE SOCIAL ASPECT OF PERSONALITY

Human beings are social beings. They work together for the benefit of society. They have fought together in time of national emergencies in order to preserve the kind of society they believe in, and they play together. While all this may be true, the social aspect of personality still is quite vague and confusing as far as some individuals are concerned.

It was a relatively easy matter to identify certain components of physical fitness such as strength and endurance. However, this does not necessarily hold true for components of social fitness. The components for physical fitness are the same for children as adults. On the other hand, the components of social fitness for children maybe different from the components of social fitness for adults. By some adult standards children, and particularly teenagers, might be considered social misfits because some of their behaviors might not be socially acceptable to some adults.

To the chagrin of some adults, parents as well as teachers, children and teenagers are likely to be uninhibited as far as the social aspect of personality is concerned. In this regard we need to be concerned with maturity as it pertains to the growing and ever changing individual. This is to say that we need to give consideration to certain characteristics of social maturity and how well they are dealt with at the different stages of growth and development of children and youth.

Perhaps we need to ask ourselves such questions as these: Are we helping children and youth to become self-reliant by giving them independence at the proper time? Are we helping them to be outgoing and interested in others as well as themselves? Are we helping them to know how to satisfy their own needs in a socially desirable way? Are we helping them to develop a wholesome attitude toward themselves and others?

Social maturity and hence social fitness might well be expressed in terms of fulfillment of certain social needs. In other words, if certain social needs are being adequately met, children and youth should be in a better position to realize social fitness. Among the needs we must give considerations to are (1) the *need for affection* which involves acceptance and approval by persons, (2) *the need for belonging* which involves acceptance and approval of the group, and (3) the *need for mutuality* which involves cooperation, mutual helpfulness, and group loyalty,

When it comes to evaluating the social aspect of personality we do not have the same kind of objective and calibrated instruments that are available in assessing the physical aspect of personality. Mainly for diagnostic purposes in their dealings with students some teachers have successfully used some of the sociometric techniques. At best, however, the social aspect of personality is difficult to appraise objectively because of its somewhat nebulous nature.

## SOCIAL OBJECTIVES

The school athletic "laboratory" (areas where activities take place) should present near ideal surroundings and environment for the social development of young people. Why are people in the field of athletics convinced that this area of the school program provides some of the very best means for teaching vital social skills? By their very nature athletic activities are essentially socially oriented. The team sports are obviously so, but so too are activities like gymnastics, swimming, tennis and golf. It is important to note that when students engage in athletics, they will be participating actually in social experiences. If any type of play is to be successful and satisfying, the people involved must possess or acquire considerable skill in dealing with one another. They must learn to work together in the interest of the team. They must learn to accept and respect the rules of the games that they play. They must learn that sometimes it is necessary to place the welfare of the team ahead of their own personal desires. They must respect the rights of others. They must be loyal to their group. They must think and plan with the group and for the group. They must learn to win and lose gracefully.

In looking back over this list of social skills that are "musts" in athletic activities, it should be discerned that it is just such social skills which are necessary for happy and successful social living everywhere. A certain level of social skills on the part of each performer is absolutely essential if play is to be successful. Everyone knows, for example, what the effects of a "poor sport" are upon a friendly game. A qualified coach finds numerous opportunities to develop skills of interpersonal relationships which far exceed the basic essentials for successful play. Indeed, men and women coaches should consider the development of increased social awareness and social skills as important objectives of their programs, and they should make specific plans to reach these objectives. They should recognize that athletic activities can have a profoundly humanizing effect upon people, in that participants quickly learn to evaluate their teammates and opponents on the basis of what they can do and what kinds of persons they are rather than on the basis of their looks, their race, their religion, their color, or their economic status.

## THE EMOTIONAL ASPECT OF PERSONALITY

In introducing the subject of emotion we are confronted with the fact that for many years it has been a difficult concept to define and in addition there have been many changing ideas and theories as far as the study of emotion is concerned.

Obviously, it is not the purpose of a book of this nature to attempt to go into any great depth on a subject that has been one of the most intricate undertakings of psychology for many years. A few general statements relative to the nature of emotion do appear to be in order if we are to understand more clearly this aspect of personality as it concerns athletics.

Emotion may be described as a response a person makes to a stimulus for which he or she is not prepared or which suggest a possible source of gain or loss. For example, if an individual is confronted with a situation and does not have a satisfactory response, the emotional pattern of fear may result; if a person is in a position where desires are frustrated, the emotional pattern of anger may occur.

This line of thought suggest that emotions might be classified in two different ways – those which are *pleasant* and those which are *unpleasant*. For example, *joy* could be considered a pleasant emotional experience while *fear* would be an unpleasant one. It is interesting to note that a good proportion of the literature is devoted to emotions that are unpleasant. It has been found that in psychology textbooks much more space is given to such emotional patterns as fear, hate, guilt, and anxiety than to such pleasant emotions as love, sympathy, and contentment.

Generally speaking, the pleasantness or unpleasantness of an emotion seems to be determined by its strength or intensity, by the nature of the situation arousing it, and by the way an individual perceives or interprets the situation. As far as young children are concerned, their emotions tend to be more intense than those of adults. If an adult is not aware of this aspect of child behavior, he or she will not likely understand why a child may react rather violently to a situation that to an adult seems somewhat insignificant. The fact that different individuals will react differently to the same type of situation also should be taken into account; for example, something that might anger one person might have a rather passive influence on another individual. In this regard, it is interesting to observe the effect that winning or losing a game has on certain individuals.

When we attempt to evaluate the emotional aspect of personality, we tend to encounter much the same situation as when we attempt to evaluate the social aspect; perhaps the emotional aspect is even more difficult to evaluate than the social aspect. Included among some of the methods used for attempting to measure emotional responses are the following:

1. *Blood pressure.* It rises when one is under some sort of emotional stress.
2. *Blood sugar analysis.* Under stressful conditions more sugar enters the blood stream.
3. *Pulse rate.* Emotional stress causes it to elevate.
4. *Galvanic skin response.* Similar to the lie detector technique and measurements recorded in terms of perspiration on palms of hands.

These as well as others have been used by investigators of human emotion and they have various and perhaps limited degrees of validity. In attempting to assess emotional reactivity we often encounter the problem of the extent to which we are dealing with a purely physiological response or a purely emotional response. For example, one's pulse rate could be elevated by taking some sort of physical exercise. It could likewise be elevated if a person were the object of an embarrassing remark by another. Thus in this illustration the elevation of pulse could be caused for different reasons, the first being physiological and the second being emotional. Then too, the type of emotional pattern is not identified by the measuring device. A joy response and an anger response could show the same or nearly the same rise impulse rate. These are some of the reasons why it is most difficult to arrive at a high degree of objectivity in studying the emotional aspect of personality.

## EMOTIONAL OBJECTIVE

Most everyone recognizes that athletic contests are highly emotionalized situations for both participants and spectators. For the participant, there is the excitement before a contest. When play is in progress there is the thrill of making skillful moves and plays, and the disappointments at being frustrated or bested by an opponent. Finally, the after-play emotions determined to some extent by how well the participant performed in relation to how well he or she thinks they can perform, but in almost all instances the pleasurable emotions caused by the good feeling that the time has been well spent. As for the spectator, he or she is likely to be swept by powerful feelings of excitement, joy, anger, and disappointments from the start to the finish of a good contest. Many sociologists are tending to believe that spectators find in their favorite sport some of the thrills, excitements, triumphs that are missing from the rest of their lives, and thus sports are of great importance to them.

From the point of view of athletic objectives there is at least one very important thing that might well be accomplished as far as the emotional aspect of personality is concerned. That is, to develop in students an increased capacity to control their emotions, *both as participants and as spectators*, and thus contributing to the development of emotional maturity.

**Emotional Control**

It could be said that the major difference between you and some criminals confined to prison is that you have the ability to control your emotional impulses to a greater extent than they. Perhaps all of us at one time or another have experienced the same kinds of emotions that have led the abnormal individual to commit violence, but we have been able to hold our powerful and violent emotions in check. This may be an extreme example but it should suggest something of the importance of emotional control in modern society.

It would appear that a reasonable and natural objective of athletics should be to help participants increase their capacity to handle and control their emotions. The thoughtful coach is aware of educational opportunities offered in athletic situations for people, both as participants and spectators, to learn to deal with their own emotional arousals in *socially acceptable ways*. He or she can try to guide students ins such a way that they learn to take pride in their ability to restrain themselves when necessary in order to abide by the rules of fair play and to behave like reasonable and decent human beings. The coach has real emotionally charged situations with which to work in order to teach young people to deal with strong emotions. Unfortunately, it cannot be said unequivocally that all coaches are taking very great advantage of an excellent opportunity. For example, one of my studies concerning spectator problems in high schools indicated that the behavior of the coach during games is one of the main things that determines how spectators behave.[3]

Another aspect of controlling the emotions is becoming able to function effectively and intelligently in an emotionally charged situation. Athletic success hinges upon this ability as does success in many other life situations. Extreme of emotional upset must be avoided if the individual is to be able to think and act effectively. In athletic situations young people should learn that if they immediately put their minds to work on other things, such as team strategy, they can then control their emotions.

It is sometimes helpful to visualize your emotions as being forces within you which are in a struggle for power with your mind as to which is to control you, your reason or your emotions. Often times our basic emotions are blind and unconcerned with the welfare of other people or sometimes even with our own welfare. Emotional maturity has to do with gaining increased mastery over our emotions – not, of course, eliminating them – so that we may behave as intelligent and civilized human beings rather than as savages or children in temper tantrums.

In summarizing emotional objectives of athletics, it could be said that these objectives should imply that sympathetic guidance should be provided in meeting anxieties, joys, and sorrows, and help given in developing aspirations, affections, and security.

## THE INTELLECTUAL ASPECT OF PERSONALITY

The word intelligence is derived from the Latin word *intellectus* which literally means the "power of knowing." One general description of it is the capacity to learn or understand.

Individuals possess varying degrees of intelligence, with most people falling within a range of what is called "normal" intelligence. In dealing with this aspect of personality we should perhaps give attention to what might be considered as some components of *intellectual fitness*. However, this is difficult to do. Because of the somewhat vague nature of intelligence, it is

---

[3] Humphrey, James H., *Sports for Children: A Guide for Adults*, Springfield, IL, Charles C. Thomas Publisher, 1993, p. 127.

practically impossible to identify specific components of it; hence, we need to view intellectual fitness in a somewhat different manner.

For purposes of this discussion, I will consider intellectual fitness from two different, but closely related points of view. First, from a standpoint of intellectual *needs* and second, from a standpoint of how certain things *influence* intelligence. It might be said that if a person's intellectual needs are being met, then he or she is intellectually fit. From the second point of view, if we know how certain things influence intelligence then we might understand better how to contribute to intellectual fitness by improving upon some of these factors.

There appears to be some rather general agreement with regard to the intellectual needs of human beings. Among others, these needs include (1) a need for challenging experiences at the individual's level of ability, (2) a need for intellectually successful and satisfying experiences, (3) a need for the opportunity to solve problems, and (4) a need for the opportunity to participate in creative experiences instead of always having to conform.

Some of those factors which tend to influence intelligence are (1) health and physical condition, (2) emotional disturbance, and (3) certain social and economic factors.

When coaches have a realization of intellectual needs and factors influencing intelligence, perhaps then they can deal satisfactorily with student athletes in helping them in their intellectual pursuits.

## INTELLECTUAL OBJECTIVES

Of the contributions that athletics might make to the development of total personality, the one concerned with intellectual development has been subjected to a certain degree of criticism by some general educators. Close scrutiny of the possibilities of intellectual development through athletics reveals, however, that a very desirable contribution can be made through this medium. This belief is substantiated in part by the affirmations of such prominent philosophers and educators as Plato, Locke, Rousseau, Pestalozzi, and numerous others. Plato's postulation that learning could take place better through play, Locke's thoughts on a sound mind and sound body, Rousseau's belief that everyone should receive plenty of wholesome physical activity early in life, and Pestalozzi's observations that students approach their studies with greater amount of interest after engaging in enjoyable physical activity, have all contributed to the modern idea that athletics and intellectual development might well be closely associated.

In a well-coached athletic activity there are numerous opportunities to exercise judgment and resort to reflective thinking in the solution of various kinds of problems. In addition, individuals must acquire a knowledge of certain rules and regulations in various kinds of games. It is also essential for effective participation that individuals gain an understanding of the various fundamentals and strategy involved in the performance of athletic activities. Perhaps of more importance is the fact that all of the systems of perception are inherent in most athletic experiences. This means that these experiences provide for improvement upon such perceptual-motor qualities as auditory and visual perception skills and kinesthetic and tactile perception skills.

In summary, there is no question that the development of a sound philosophy and the formulation of valid objectives is perhaps the most important aspect of a successful interscholastic athletic program. It is hoped that the suggestions set forth in this chapter will be of use to those individuals who have major responsibilities in this area.

*Chapter 3*

# FUNCTIONS OF THE ATHLETIC DIRECTOR

To suggest that the job of the secondary school athletic director is comparable to that of a corporate chief executive officer perhaps could be considered by some as a gross exaggeration. Nonetheless, they often times are confronted with the same types of problems: budgetary woes, facilities and equipment concerns, hiring and firing and the like. In addition, more often than not, they have to deal with over zealous parents who have the mistaken notion that their son or daughter is a potential All-American or World Record Holder.

Just what do persons responsible for directing interscholastic athletics do on the job? This was information that I considered essential as a part of an effective data base for this book. Therefore, it was for this reason that I conducted a nationwide job analysis study of several hundred secondary school athletic directors.

Job analysis, the process of determining and reporting upon the pertinent information relating to the nature of specific jobs is not new. As far back as 1619 a Committee within the Virginia Colony of London was appointed to describe the duties of the several officers of the company.

Leaders in business and industry have long been aware of the importance of job analysis as a basis for deciding upon the type and extend of training necessary to prepare persons for certain jobs in the business and industrial world.

The technique of job analysis has been adopted from business and industry by many of the professions with the field of education experiencing some satisfying results. Thus, there was a very good reason to believe that a job analysis in the area of secondary school athletic administration could produce important findings. My own personal experience in job analysis research facilitated my efforts in this regard since I had previously conducted job analyses of public school physical education directors and public school health education supervisors.

In the current study I found that the functions which the secondary school athletic director may be called upon to perform comprise an almost unbelievable range of activities. Indeed, if a secondary school athletic director were to attain the status of an expert in all of the extensive variety of duties related to his or her position, he or she could undoubtedly be classified as a universal genius. The impact of this statement will perhaps be more fully appreciated upon examination of the many functions performed by secondary school athletic directors.

## THE RATING SCALE

*The Humphrey Job Analysis Scale* was developed by means of documentary analysis, personal logs and diaries, personal interviews, and introspection. These procedures yielded more than 250 duties that might be performed by secondary school athletic directors. By means of combining, recombining, condensing, and telescoping there evolved a final list of 64 duties, all of which will be identified later in the chapter.

### Criteria for Rating the Duties

The criteria for rating the duties were: (1) frequency of performance of the duty, (2) degree of difficulty of the duty, and (3) degree of importance of the duty.

*Frequency of Performance*
Frequency was considered on the basis of a quantitative range. The reason for this was that such quantita-terms as *daily*, *weekly*, etc., would make no allowance, for example, for a duty performed more often than once a week

and less often than once a day. Thus, the participants were asked to rate the duties in the following manner.

Rate all of the duties for frequency by circling the number in the frequency column which best describes the frequency with which the duty is performed by you personally.

| | | |
|---|---|---|
| 4 | Very Frequently | A duty performed once or more a week |
| 3 | Frequently | A duty performed once or more in two weeks but not as often as once a week |
| 2 | Occasionally | A duty performed once or more a month but not as often as once in two weeks |
| 1 | Infrequently | A duty which is performed once or twice a year |
| x | Not Performed | A duty which you do not perform personally in your position |

*Difficulty*

It was not the purpose of this study to determine *why* certain duties are more difficult to perform than others. Often times a duty may not be difficult to perform but certain contingencies can make it so. For example, such factors as time constraints and lack of cooperation on the part of school officials could increase the difficulty of certain duties. The following directions and rating scale were used for this purpose.

Rate those duties for difficult which you perform by circling the number in the difficulty column which best describes the degree of difficulty in terms of obtaining desired results.

| | |
|---|---|
| 4 | extreme |
| 3 | considerable |
| 2 | moderate |
| 1 | some |
| x | none |

*Importance*

The importance of a duty should be determined by the application of carefully validated objectives. Participants were requested to rate the duties for importance as follows:

Rate all of the duties for importance by circling the number in the importance column which best describes the degree of importance which you attach to the duty. This should be in terms of how important you consider the duty to be in reaching your objectives.

| | |
|---|---|
| 4 | extreme |
| 3 | considerable |
| 2 | moderate |
| 1 | some |
| x | none |

## CLASSIFICATION OF DUTIES

After the final list of duties was compiled the next step was to place them in classifications. This was done arbitrarily with the duties classified as follows: (1) administrative duties; (2) duties pertaining to facilities and equipment; (3) duties pertaining to athletic contests; (4) duties pertaining to coaching and coaches; (5) duties pertaining to student athletes; and (6) duties pertaining to community and public relations.

Although no claims are made as to perfection of classification, the duties seemed to fit well into most of the classifications given above. In some instances certain duties seemed to fit equally well into more than one classification and a certain amount of overlapping also seemed unavoidable.

### Administrative Duties

Athletics in the public schools involves many responsibilities, not the least of which are the numerous problems concerned with organization and administration. Athletic directors sometimes complain of the many administrative details involved in carrying out the program. Many of these functions may perhaps be considered by some to be routine and unimportant, but they may, nevertheless, be essential to the success of the program. The following list enumerates a variety of administrative duties of personnel for directing the athletic program. (Incidentally, it should be noticed that the percent of the athletic directors participating in a specific duty is shown in parenthesis for each of the duties. This information can be important to the reader when observing the data presented about frequency, difficulty, and importance later in the chapter.)

1. Attend to office routine necessary to performance of duties such as correspondence, etc. (100)
2. Prepare notices and announcements. (100)
3. Conduct staff meetings. (100)
4. Have conferences with and make reports to superiors. (100)
5. Prepare budget and receipt of expenditures of athletic teams. (98)
6. Prepare and administer various supplemental athletic program budgets. (85)
7. Coordinate involvement and collection of monies for fund-raising activities as it pertains to athletics. (81)
8. Handle ticket sales and gate receipts for athletic teams. (87)
9. Schedule game supervisors and ticket takers. (91)
10. Coordinate activities of cheerleaders, bands, etc..as they pertain to athletics. (87)
11. Develop criteria, procedures, and instruments necessary to effectively evaluate the interscholastic program. (98)

## Duties Pertaining to Facilities and Equipment

As used here the term *facilities* refers to permanent types of structures: *equipment* generally concerns a variety of items somewhat less permanent than facilities. Some of these duties performed by athletic directors follow.

1. Coordinate the inspection of all athletic facilities and equipment which may be used to insure safety of spectators and contestants. (100)
2. Supervise sanitary conditions of athletic facilities. (89)

3. Schedule practice areas for activities occurring at the same time. (98)
4. Coordinate practice schedules for field and building use. (98)
5. Coordinate use of athletic facilities and equipment by outside groups. (89)
6. Provide plan for issue and return of equipment used by athletes. (85)
7. Supervise arrangements for cleaning, repairing, and maintaining of all uniforms and equipment. (81)
8. Prepare purchase orders and purchase new equipment. (94)
9. Keep an accurate inventory of all athletic equipment. (89)
10. Participate in planning of new facilities. (91)

## Duties Pertaining to Athletic Contests

A good proportion of an athletic director's responsibilities are concerned with the conduct of various contests. Following are some of the duties performed in this classification.

1. Schedule contests for athletic teams. (100)
2. Make preparations for home athletic contests including facilities, advertising, etc. (100)
3. Arrange for transportation for athletic teams. (96)
4. Prepare contracts for athletic teams. (87)
5. Arrange for police, ambulance, and other public safety departments to have representatives at home athletic contests, if necessary. (98)
6. Prepare list of approved officials. (68)
7. Submit athletic schedule to appropriate person(s) for assignment of officials. (91)
8. Be responsible for obtaining officials of all athletic contests. (85)
9. Advise officials associations of postponements, rescheduling and/or cancellation of athletic contests. (100)
10. Scout interscholastic contests. (21)
11. Keep a record of the results of all athletic contests (score, expense, etc...) (79)

## Duties Pertaining to Coaching and Coaches

It is obvious that any administrator will have personnel to deal with and of course this is the case with secondary school athletic directors. It is interesting to note that almost one third of the participants in my study also served as head coach of a varsity sport - ordinarily football. I have queried several school superintendents about such a dual responsibility. Sometimes they feel that a higher salary is justified by having one person in two such positions.

1. Coach interscholastic team(s). (32)
2. Assistant coach of interscholastic team(s). (15)
3. Interview prospective coaches. (100)
4. Assist principal and/or superintendent in selecting and assigning coaches. (94)
5. Orient new coaches into the school system. (98)
6. See that all coaches receive from each athlete participation and medical permits from parents and doctors prior to taking part in any practice session. (96)
7. Coordinate care and prevention of athletic injuries course for coaches and Certify course completion. (74)
8. Provide inservice programs for new coaches. (83)
9. See that all coaches, at the end of each sport season, submit updated inventory and budget requests for the following year. (94)
10. Assist the principal and/or superintendent in evaluating coaches. (95)

## Duties Pertaining to Student Athletes

Since the students are the most important persons in the program, the athletic director has a number of functions to perform in this classification. Some of these types of duties are identified in the following list.

1. Verify the eligibility of each athlete. (96)
2. Monitor and report academic ineligibility of athletes. (96)

3. Keep a record of proof of age of each candidate for each athletic activity. (81)
4. Arrange for excuses for athletes for game participation. (68)
5. Develop a plan for athletic awards. (89)
6. Make arrangements for the physical examination of each candidate for each athletic activity. (66)
7. Develop plan for accident insurance for athletes. (64)
8. Keep a file of physical examination results for all students who participate in the interscholastic program. (91)
9. Develop procedures with coaches for handling athletic injuries with specific consideration for those who are recovering from injury. (77)
10. Require written permission from parents of all students before permitting them to practice for interscholastic competition. (89)
11. Organize and administer athletic team substance abuse awareness and prevention. (77)
12. Make home visits regarding athletes. (30)

## Duties Pertaining to Community and Public Relations

In general, all school personnel are expected to participate to some extent in community activities. Because of the nature of the work, the athletic director will, perhaps, engage in a variety of community functions. This is important if all community resources are to be utilized to meet the needs of students. The following functions involving community and public relations have been identified as those in which secondary school athletic directors are likely to engage.

1. Provide a plan for public relations for your department. (91)
2. Approve all press releases concerning the athletic program. (70)
3. Act as a school liaison to media. (85)
4. Conduct school TV program. (11)
5. Supervise internet website. (21)
6. Act in an advisory capacity with athletic booster clubs. (89)
7. Address numerous community groups about school athletics. (85)

8. Develop plan for community professional personnel in school athletics such as physicians. (70)
9. Act as school liaison to local youth groups. (68)
10. Attend professional meetings to keep informed of the research and developments in interscholastic athletics. (100)

## Other Duties Performed by Secondary School

*Athletic Directors*

It should be kept in mind that theoretical completeness has not been assumed so far as the various duties are concerned. In analyzing the functions performed by the athletic director, specific duties have been identified which are peculiar to this type of position. If all of the duties were collected, they would, no doubt, equal the number of activities engaged in by anyone throughout a lifetime. However, many of these which may be of a sporadic nature could perhaps be incorporated into the functions listed on the previous pages. In any event, the duties set forth in this chapter should give the reader an appreciation of the functions of the secondary school athletic director.

In summarizing this section of the chapter, certain additional job-related matters should be taken into account. For one thing, the athletic directors were preponderantly male with only eight percent of females among the participants in my study.

In most instances the athletic director had various duties other than those directly related to athletics. In fact, only about five percent of the directors spent all of their time on athletics. Many of them also directed the physical education program, driver education and the like as well as carrying a teaching load. The following tabulation gives a clearer indication of the actual time spent on duties other than those concerned with athletics.

| Percent of Directors | Percent of Time Spent on Other Duties |
| --- | --- |
| 5 | 0 |
| 27 | 5-10 |
| 28 | 25-30 |
| 26 | 40-50 |
| 14 | more than 50 |

Almost seven percent of the athletic directors also served as an assistant principal.

In the latter position they also assumed duties involving curriculum, discipline, and staff evaluation.

At the risk one takes in dealing with norms, I would like to submit the following profile of the average athletic director according to my study: A male with 10 years experience in a school with 9-12 grade levels and an enrollment of 1300 pupils. He presides over both boys' and girls' programs and supervises 10-15 sports. Finally, he spends about 25 to 30 percent of his time in duties that are not directly related to athletics.

Considering the innumerable duties the athletic director is called upon to perform and the responsibility he or she must assumes, it is a position that could induce any number of stress-inducing situations. And, this subject as it pertains to secondary school athletic directors is addressed in the final chapter.

## RANK ORDER OF FREQUENCY, DIFFICULTY AND IMPORTANCE OF DUTIES

The rest of this chapter is devoted to the order of frequency, difficulty, and importance of the duties as rated by the participants in my study. The number in parenthesis before each duty is an average of all ratings. For example, the figure 2.50 for frequency would translate into *occasionally* to *frequently*.

## Rank Order of Frequency

1. (3.83) Attend to office routine necessary to performance of duties such as correspondence, etc...
2. (3.74) Make preparations for home athletic contests including preparation of facilities, advertising, etc...
3. (3.63) Arrange for transportation for athletic teams.
4. (3.62) Schedule contests for athletic teams
5. (3.60) Verify the eligibility of each athlete.
6. (3.55) Schedule game supervisors and ticket takers.
7. (3.51) Handle ticket sales and gate receipts for athletic teams.
8. (3.44) See that all coaches receive from each athlete participation and medical permits from parents and doctors prior to taking part in any practice session.
9. (3.49) Monitor and report academic ineligibility of athletes.
10. (3.41) Prepare purchase orders and purchase new equipment.
11. (3.40) Coach interscholastic team(s).
12. (3.36) Require written permission from parents of all students before permitting them to practice for interscholastic competition.
13. (3.30) Prepare notices and announcements.
14. (3.29) Prepare contracts for athletic teams.
15. (3.29) Act in advisory capacity with athletic booster clubs.
16. (3.26) Advise officials associations of postponements, rescheduling and/or cancellation of athletic contests.
17. (3.24) Be responsible for obtaining officials for all athletic contests.
18. (3.21) Keep a file of physical examination results for all students who participate in the interscholastic program.
19. (3.20) Schedule practice areas for activities occurring at the same time.
20. (3.20) Coordinate practice schedules for field and building use.
21. (3.14) Submit athletic schedule to appropriate persons(s) for assignment of officials.
22. (3.04) Assist the principal and/or superintendent in evaluating coaches.

23. (3.02) See that all coaches, at the end of each sport season, submit updated inventory and budget requests for the following school year.
24. (3.00) Assistant coach of interscholastic teams(s).
25. (2.98) Arrange for police, ambulance, and other public safety departments to have representatives at home athletic contests, if necessary.
26. (2.93) Keep a record of proof of age of each candidate for each athletic activity.
27. (2.87) Interview prospective coaches.
28. (2.86) Assist principal and/or superintendent in selecting and assigning coaches.
29. (2.85) Arrange for excuses for athletes for game participation.
30. (2.81) Coordinate use of athletic facilities and equipment by outside groups.
31. (2.80) Prepare budget and receipt of expenditures for athletic teams.
32. (2.80) Orient new coaches into the school system.
33. (2.79) Coordinate care and prevention of athletic injuries course for coaches and certify course completion.
34. (2.78) Prepare list of approved officials.
35. (2.78) Act as school liaison to media.
36. (2.77) Coordinate the inspection of all athletic facilities and equipment which may be used to insure safety of spectators and contestants.
37. (2.68) Have conferences with and make reports to superiors.
38. (2.68) Keep an accurate inventory of all athletic equipment.
39. (2.67) Supervise internet web site.
40. (2.63) Attend professional meetings to keep informed of the research and developments in interscholastic athletics.
41. (2.61) develop procedures with coaches for handling athletic injuries with specific consideration for those who are recovering from injury.
42. (2.60) Keep a record of the results of all athletic contests (score, expenses, etc.).
43. (2.58) Provide plan for public relations for your department.

44. (2.56) Coordinate activities of cheerleaders, bands, etc…as they pertain to athletics.
45. (2.52) Provide plan for issue and return of equipment used by athletes.
46. (2.47) Supervise arrangements for cleaning, repairing and maintaining of all uniforms and equipment.
47. (2.45) Develop a plan for athletic awards.
48. (2.42) Organize and administer athletic team substance abuse awareness and prevention.
49. (2.37) Develop plan for accident insurance for athletes.
50. (2.36) Provide in service program for new coaches.
51. (2.36) Approve all press releases concerning the athletic program.
52. (2.30) Act as school liaison to local youth groups.
53. (2.28) Prepare and administer various supplemental athletic program budgets.
54. (2.25) Make arrangements for the physical examination of each candidate for each athletic activity.
55. (2.24) Coordinate involvement and collection of monies for fund-raising activities as it pertains to athletics.
56. (2.18) Develop plan for community professional personnel in school athletics such as physicians.
57. (2.13) Develop criteria, procedures, and instruments necessary to effectively evaluate the interscholastic program.
58. (2.13) Address numerous community groups about school athletics.
59. (2.12) Participation in planning of new facilities.
60. (2.12) Supervise sanitary conditions of athletic facilities.
61. (2.02) Conduct staff meetings.
62. (1.46) Conduct school TV programs.
63. (1.36) Make home visits regarding athletes.
64. (0.51) Scout interscholastic contests.

## Rank Order of Difficulty

1. Coach interscholastic teams(s).
2. (2.91) Prepare budget and receipt of expenditures for athletic teams.
3. (2.83) Make preparation for home athletic contests including preparation of facilities, advertising, etc…
4. (2.83) See that all coaches receive from each athlete participation and medical permits from parents and doctors prior to taking part in any practice session.
5. (2.82) Verify the eligibility of each athlete.
6. (2.81) See that all coaches, at the end of each sport season, submit updated inventory and budget requests for the following school year.
7. (2.76) Schedule contests for athletic teams.
8. (2.76) Assist the principal and/or superintendent in evaluating coaches.
9. (2.69) Coordinate care and prevention of athletic injuries course and certify course completion.
10. (2.67) Assist principal and/or superintendent in selecting and assigning coaches.
11. (2.64) Monitor and report academic ineligibility of athletes.
12. (2.62) Develop criteria, procedures, and instruments necessary to effectively evaluate the interscholastic program.
13. (2.60) Coordinate practice schedules for field and building us.
14. (2.60) Orient new coaches into the school system.
15. (2.59) Interview prospective coaches.
16. (2.54) Schedule practice areas for activities occurring at the same time.
17. (2.54) Require written permission from parents of all students before permitting to practice for interscholastic competition.
18. (2.54) Organize and administer team substance abuse awareness and prevention.
19. (2.53) Keep an accurate inventory of all athletic equipment.
20. (2.52) Advise officials associations of postponements, rescheduling, and/or cancellation of athletic contests.
21. (2.42) Schedule game supervisors and ticket takers.

22. (2.42) Participate in planning of new facilities.
23. (2.42) Arrange for transportation of athletic teams.
24. (2.40) Provide plan for public relations for your department.
25. (2.38) Coordinate the inspection of all athletic facilities and equipment which may be used to insure safety of spectators and contestants.
26. (2.37) Prepare and administer various supplemental athletic program budgets.
27. (2.36) Prepare purchase orders and purchase new equipment.
28. (2.35) Be responsible for obtaining officials for all athletic contests.
29. (2.35) Make arrangements for the physical examination of each candidate for each athletic activity.
30. (2.35) Develop plan for community professional personnel in school athletics such as physicians.
31. (2.33) Develop procedures with coaches for handling athletic injuries with specific consideration for those who are recovering from injury.
32. (2.31) Keep a file of physical examination results for all student who participate in the interscholastic program.
33. (2.31) Make home visits regarding athletes.
34. (2.30) Coordinate use of athletic facilities and equipment by outside groups.
35. (2.27) Keep a record of proof of age of each candidate for each athletic activity.
36. (2.24) Conduct staff meetings.
37. (2.24) Submit athletic schedule to appropriate person(s) for assignment of officials.
38. (2.23) Develop a plan for athletic awards.
39. (2.23) Act in advisory capacity with athletic booster clubs.
40. (2.21) Attend professional meetings to keep informed of the research and developments in interscholastic athletics.
41. (2.21) Supervise arrangements for cleaning, repairing, and maintaining all uniforms and equipment.
42. (2.21) Prepare list of approved officials.
43. (2.21) Develop plan for accident insurance for athletes.

44. (2.21) Provide plan for issue and return of equipment used by athletes.
45. (2.17) Assistant coach of interscholastic team(s).
46. (2.13) Arrange for police, ambulance, and other public safety departments to have representatives at home athletic contests, if necessary.
47. (2.13) Keep a record of the results of all athletic contests (score, expenses, etc...).
48. (2.11) Have conferences with and make reports to supervisors.
49. (2.10) Supervise internet website.
50. (2.09) Attend to office routine necessary to performance of duties such as correspondence, etc...
51. (2.09) Supervise sanitary conditions of athletic facilities.
52. (2.08) Prepare contracts for athletic teams.
53. (2.06) Arrange for excuses for athletes for game participation.
54. (2.05) Act as school liaison to media.
55. (2.03) Approve all press releases concerning the athletic program.
56. (1.98) Coordinate involvement and collection of monies for fund-raising activities as it pertains to athletics.
57. (1.98) Handle ticket sales and gate receipts for athletic teams.
58. (1.97) Act as school liaison to local youth groups.
59. (1.95) Address numerous community groups about school athletics.
60. (1.93) Coordinate activities of cheerleaders, bands, etc... as they pertain to athletics.
61. (1.93) Scout interscholastic contests.
62. (1.84) Provide in service programs for new coaches.
63. (1.69) Prepare notices and announcements.
64. (1.20) Attend professional meetings to keep informed of the research and developments in interscholastic athletics.

## Rank Order of Importance

1. Schedule contests for athletic teams.
2. (3.84) Monitor and report academic ineligibility of athletes.
3. (3.81) Verify the eligibility of each athlete.
4. (3.76) Prepare budget and receipt of expenditures of athletic teams.
5. (3.75) Arrange for transportation of athletic teams.
6. (3.73) See that all coaches receive from each athlete participation and medical permits from parents and doctors prior to taking part in any practice session.
7. (3.72) Interview prospective coaches.
8. (3.70) Assist the principal and/or superintendent in evaluating coaches.
9. (3.68) Make arrangements for the physical examination of each candidate for each athletic activity.
10. (3.66) Submit athletic schedule to appropriate person(s) for assignment of officials.
11. (3.66) Assist principal and/or superintendent in selecting and assigning coaches.
12. (3.66) Coordinate care and prevention of athletic injuries course for coaches and certify course completion.
13. (3.66) Keep a file of physical examination results for all students who participate in the interscholastic program.
14. (3.66) Require written permission form parents of all students before permitting them to practice for interscholastic competition.
15. (3.63) Advise officials association of postponements, rescheduling and/or cancellation of athletic contests.
16. (3.61) Prepare purchase orders and purchase new equipment.
17. (3.60) Make preparation for home athletic contests including preparation of facilities, advertising, etc…
18. (3.58) Coordinate the inspection of all athletic facilities and equipment which may be used to insure safety of spectators and contestants.
19. (3.58) Keep an accurate inventory of all athletic equipment.

20. (3.56) Keep a record of proof of age of each candidate for each athletic activity.
21. (3.56) Organize and administer athletic team substance abuse awareness and prevention.
22. (3.51) Orient new coaches into the school system.
23. (3.50) Coach interscholastic team(s).
24. (3.49) Attend to office routine necessary to performance of duties such as correspondence.
25. (3.47) Arrange for police, ambulance, and other public safety departments to have representatives at home athletic contests, if necessary.
26. (3.47) Attend professional meetings to keep informed of the research and developments in interscholastic athletics.
27. (3.45) Prepare contracts for athletic teams.
28. (3.45) See that all coaches, at the end of each sport season, submit updated inventory and budget requests for the following school year.
29. (3.45) Arrange for excuses for athletes for game participation.
30. (3.43) Be responsible for obtaining officials for all athletic contests.
31. (3.39) Schedule practice areas for activities occurring at the same time.
32. (3.37) Schedule game supervisors and ticket takers.
33. (3.34) Coordinate practice schedule for field and building use.
34. (3.34) Provide in service program for new coaches.
35. (3.31) Develop procedures with coaches for handling athletic injuries with specific consideration for those who are recovering from injury.
36. (3.29) Supervise sanitary conditions of athletic facilities.
37. (3.28) Prepare notices and announcements.
38. (3.28) Act in advisory capacity with athletic booster clubs.
39. (3.25) Provide plan for issue and return of equipment used by athletes.
40. (3.25) Develop plan for athletic awards.
41. (3.22) Develop plan for accident insurance for athletes.
42. (3.21) Have conferences with and make reports to superiors.
43. (3.21) Provide plan for public relations for your department.

44. (3.20) Prepare and administer various supplemental athletic program budgets.
45. (3.20) Handle ticket sales and gate receipts for athletic teams.
46. (3.19) Participate in planning of new facilities.
47. (3.18) Supervise arrangements for cleaning, repairing, and maintaining of all uniforms and equipment.
48. (3.12) Conduct staff meetings.
49. (3.10) Supervise internet website.
50. (3.07) Develop criteria, procedures, and instruments necessary to effectively evaluate the interscholastic program.
51. (3.06) Prepare list of approved officials.
52. (3.00) Assistant coach of interscholastic team(s).
53. (2.97) Approve all press releases concerning the athletic teams.
54. (2.92) Address numerous community groups about school athletics.
55. (2.89) Keep a record of the results of all athletic contests (score, expenses, etc…).
56. (2.88) Develop plan for community professional personnel in school athletics such as physicians.
57. (2.88) Coordinate use of athletic facilities and equipment by outside groups.
58. (2.77) Act as school liaison to local youth groups.
59. (2.76) Coordinate involvement and collection of monies for fund-raising activities as it pertains to athletics.
60. (2.69) Make home visits regarding athletes.
61. (2.60) Conduct school TV program.
62. (2.48) Act as school liaison to media.
63. (2.34) Coordinate activities of cheerleaders, bands, etc…, as they pertain to athletics.
64. (2.27) Scout interscholastic contests.

In summary, although these data do not necessarily justify definitive conclusions, at the same time some reasonable speculations can be made with some degree of confidence. Some of these can be enumerated as follows.

1. The master list of duties may be considered sufficiently comprehensive with regard to the multitude of duties performed by the secondary school athletic director.

2. The master list of duties could be used for the following purposes.
   a. A checklist for persons interested in interscholastic athletics as a career.
   b. A checklist for teacher preparation institutions for determining the needs of students, especially at the graduate level.
   c. A self-analysis checklist for those in the field to expand their knowledge and interest and improve their practices.
   d. It might be useful to state departments of education as a means of developing standards to evaluate the duties of secondary school athletic directors.

*Chapter 4*

# LEADERSHIP IN INTERSCHOLASTIC ATHLETICS

It is a well-established fact that in any systematic purposeful activity one of the most important requirements is that of leadership. And, of course interscholastic athletics is no exception. It is the purpose of this chapter to take into account the leadership responsibilities of certain individuals who are involved in the educational process, particularly as it pertains to interscholastic athletics.

## THE RESPONSIBILITY FOR LEADERSHIP

The question of who shall assume a major portion of the responsibility for leadership in interscholastic athletics will depend primarily upon the size of the community as well as the number of schools in the community. The quality of leadership is not likely to be the same for small communities as for larger communities. In other words, certain conditions existing in very small communities, such as lack of funds, and limited school enrollment, will have an effect upon the extent to which specialized leadership in interscholastic athletics is available.

As a general rule, medium- and large-sized communities require athletic directors to have experience and perhaps more preparation in order to qualify for these positions.

# SCHOOL PERSONNEL RESPONSIBLE FOR LEADERSHIP IN INTERSCHOLASTIC ATHLETICS

While everyone in a specific school system is likely to be concerned with and have some degree of interest in interscholastic athletics, much of the responsibility will rest with certain school officials. In this respect the superintendent of schools, school principal, athletic director, and coach may be considered to have the greatest responsibility for a successful program in interscholastic athletics.

## Responsibility of the Superintendent of Schools

The ultimate responsibility for leadership in interscholastic athletics in public schools will rest with the superintendent of schools. The direct responsibilities the superintendent must assume will depend almost entirely upon the size of the community and the number of schools in the community. For example, in a small community with one elementary school and one high school, or one building housing all grades, the superintendent is likely to have many responsibilities in addition to his or her administrative duties. He or she may not only have the direct responsibility for interscholastic athletics, but her or she may teach some of the classes and coach athletic teams as well. This situation will generally exist only in the very small communities. For as a general rule the larger the community the smaller the amount of direct supervision of interscholastic athletics need be provided by the superintendent. Even in some of the smaller communities of the type mentioned previously, there may be a certain amount of interscholastic athletic supervision provided at the county level, thus minimizing the direct supervision for which the superintendent must be responsible.

In communities of sufficient size where the functions of the superintendent are for the most part administrative, the superintendent will probably assume little if any direct responsibility for the interscholastic athletic program. The responsibility which the administrative head of the school system assumes will be more or less of an indirect nature. That is, the superintendent will no doubt be responsible for providing the services of specialized personnel and delegating persons to assume the direct responsibility of interscholastic athletics.

The superintendent of schools should also assume a large measure of the responsibility for satisfactory organization for all phases of interscholastic athletics within the school system. If provision is made for the best organizational plan in light of the local needs, coordination of the various departments of the school system should reach the highest degree of effectiveness. This may be one of the most worthwhile contributions which the superintendent of schools can make to the successful leadership in interscholastic athletics.

The final responsibility for all aspects of the educational program will rest with the superintendent of schools. For this reason all persons employed in a specific school system will be directly or indirectly responsible to the superintendent. It has been found that the most satisfactory relationship between the superintendent and the person in charge of interscholastic athletics is when the superintendent uses the latter in an advisory capacity.

While the superintendent should be expected to have a thorough understanding of all areas of education, it is doubtful that any superintendent would qualify as an expert in all of these areas. As a consequence, the superintendent is likely to place the responsibility for interscholastic athletics on an individual especially qualified in this field. Once this individual has assumed the position he or she should be given as much freedom as possible in developing the program to the fullest extent. His or her relationship with the superintendent of schools will probably consist mainly of keeping the superintendent informed about the program. This may be done through periodic reports or occasional conference with the superintendent.

## Responsibility of the School Principal

The relationship of the person in charge of interscholastic athletics to the school principal will be of a somewhat different nature than that of this person and the superintendent. While the superintendent may delegate the responsibility of the interscholastic athletic program to an athletic director, the principal and athletic director must work in close cooperation if the program is to be carried out successfully. In fact, it might be said that one of the first prerequisites for success in the interscholastic athletic program is the mutual understanding existing between the athletic director and the principal. Because of the fact that the athletic director and the principal should work together for the ultimate benefit of students, it is very important that the relationship between these two officials be clearly defined. In this connection, it would perhaps be wise for the athletic director and the principal to set up a mutual agreement with regard to certain functions. For example, they should agree on: (1) The function each will perform without consulting the other; (2) the functions each will not perform without consulting the other; and (3) those situations which the athletic director will report to the principal in writing.

## Responsibility of the Athletic Director

A starting pint in discussing the leadership responsibility of the athletic director could begin with the professional preparation of that individual. In this regard it is very interesting to note that the National Council of Secondary School Athletic Directors (NCSSAD) directed its attention to this subject at its annual meeting in April 1999. The NCSSAD is a part of the National Association for Sports and Physical Education (NASPE) which in turn is an Association in The American Alliance for Health, Physical Education, Recreation and Dance. The subject of the Council's meeting was *So You Want to be an Athletic Director?* And was described in the following manner:

> The Executive Board of the NCSSAD will discuss a very important issue that today's athletic director must be able to manage and cope with in performing the expectations of today's athletic administrator. Professional preparation for the athletic administrator has not been an undergraduate major; many successful coaches are appointed to the task of being an athletic administrator in the secondary task of being an athletic administrator in the secondary schools of today and sometimes a "sink or swim" situation exists in that very important role.

This statement succinctly expresses the need for some sort of professional preparation. Some athletic directors have had training in the field of physical education, and, as a result may have had a course in the general area of administration. Also, more and more colleges and universities are now offering specialization in what is called "sports management." Some recent graduates may have possibly benefited from courses in this area. And, of course, athletic directors should attempt to obtain the Certified Athletic Administrator endorsement.

It would be very difficult to determine the ideal combination of preparation and experience needed by a secondary school athletic director. This is particularly true because each community has its own problems which manifest themselves in a specific manner. Nevertheless, there are certain basic fundamentals in the way of preparation which should be acquired for success. For, example, the athletic director should have knowledge of the history, principles, and philosophy of general education. This is essential if he or she is to make sound application of the principles of interscholastic athletics.

*Personal Traits of the Athletic Director*

Although the preparation of the athletic director is important, persons employed in these positions should not be selected entirely on this basis. It should be emphasized that preparation itself will not assure success. In addition to adequate preparation an athletic director must possess certain desirable personal qualities which are conducive to the human relationships involved in working with many different individuals with varying types of personalities. In fact, of the numerous factors involved in determining the success of an athletic director, personal qualities should perhaps be regarded as one of the most important.

Probably no single trait of the total number constituting the athletic director's complete personality can be said to be the most important in all cases. Generally speaking, the effectiveness of one's various personal qualities will be dependent upon the particular situation. For this reason it would perhaps follow that the athletic director endowed with the greatest number of strong personal traits will have a distinct advantage and will be more likely to succeed in relationships with co-workers.

While it does not seem possible to identify personal traits which are most important to success in interscholastic athletics, such qualities as sympathetic understanding, ability to install confidence and professional enthusiasm are but a few which should contribute to the success of the secondary school athletic director.

*Expectations of the Athletic Director*

I am sure that most of us remember the immortal words of Robert Burns:

> O wad some poser the giftie gie us
> To see oursel's as others see us!

In any case, Doug Duval, Mundelein, Illinois High School's Athletic Director decided to try to determine how others "saw the athletic director." He did this by soliciting the opinions of a number of professional educators and others. He has generously shared his findings with me and I am pleased to present a few excerpts as follows:

Bill Gorski, A U. S. history teacher as Mundelein High School:

> As a teacher I see the athletic director as a central person in the life of a high school. This person must not only be the coordinator of activities, but also a liaison between students, teachers and parents. Undoubtedly, the task is a formidable one.

Perry Wilhelm, the parent of a Mundelein High School athlete:

> The athletic director has to be many things to many different people. As a parent, one of the first things I notice about the athletic director in his visibility. Just seeing him at athletic contests, meetings, etc...lets me know his level of concern for the athletic programs. Also important is his accessibility to parents. Is he personable, approachable and friendly? Does he treat all sports equally?

Dr. Dennis Hockney, superintendent of Antioch Community High School District 117, Antioch, Illinois:

> All the qualities of athletic director noted are necessary and none is more important that the other. As a *leader* the person must have the courage to set a direction and to be out in front pulling others along. As a *relater* the person must have the people skills necessary to build positive relationships with parents, coaches, teachers, administrators athletes, reporters, etc...As a *problem-solver* the person must remain objective when confronted with problems and must gather information, involve all parties, listen weigh the facts and make a decision. Courage, once again, is a necessary trait. As a *delegator* the person must recognize that he or she cannot do it all

and delegate to those hired to perform specific responsibilities. In the end, the athletic director, like any other educational leader, must carry out his or her duties and responsibilities in a manner which results in the student-athlete having a positive learning experience.[1]

All of the above statements identify important leadership qualities of the secondary school athletic director.

And finally, an excellent criterion for leadership of the athletic director is expressed in the Athletic Administrators Code of Ethics developed by the National Interscholastic Athletic Administrators Association (NIAAA). (See Figure 2.)

## Responsibility of the Coach

Since the coach is the one nearest to the student athlete, his or her leadership is of extreme importance. The coaching profession can be characterized by its uniqueness. The coach is at once a teacher, a psychologist, a father/mother figure, and whatever else he or she needs to be at any given time.

Often times the coach and his or her leadership responsibilities are not clearly understood, particularly by some parents. Therefore, it is very important to keep communication lines open between parents and coaches. Some schools have attempted to do this and one excellent example is the "Parent/Coach Communication" developed under the leadership of Bill Sissel, Athletic Director at Hoffman Estates, Illinois High School. Following are some excerpts from the communication.

---

[1] Duval, Doug, Reflections: Who is looking at you and what do they expect to see? *Interscholastic Athletic Administration,* Spring 1999, p. 25.

## NATIONAL INTERSCHOLASTIC ATHLETIC ADMINISTRATORS ASSOCIATION CODE OF ETHICS

The Interscholastic Athletic Administrator as an Educational Leader:

a. Develops and maintains a comprehensive athletic program which seeks the highest development of all participants, and which respects the individual dignity of every athlete.
b. Considers the well-being of the entire student body as fundamental in all decisions and actions.
c. Supports the principle of due process and protects the civil and human rights of all individuals.
d. Organizes, directs and promotes an interscholastic athletic program that is an integral part of the total educational program.
e. Cooperates with the staff and school administration in establishing, implementing and supporting school policies.
f. Acts impartially in the execution of basic policies and in the enforcement of the conference, league, and state high school association rules and regulations.
g. Fulfills professional responsibilities with honesty and integrity.
h. Upholds the honor of the profession in all relations with students, colleagues, coaches, administrators and the general public.
i. Improves the professional status and effectiveness of the interscholastic administrator through participation in local, state and national in-service programs.
j. Promotes high standards of ethics, sportsmanship and personal conduct by encouraging administration, coaches, staff, student-athletes, and community to commit to these high standards.

Prepared by the NIAAA Professional Development Committee

Revised 7/94

**Figure 2.** NIAAA Athletic Administrator Code of Ethics

1. Communications You Should Expect from Your Child's Coach.
   - Philosophy of the coach
   - Expectations the coach has for your child as well as all the players on the squad.
   - Location and times of all practices and contests.
   - Team requirements, i.e., fees, special equipment, off-season conditioning.
   - Procedure should your child be injured during participation.
   - Discipline that results in the denial of your child's participation.

2. Communication Coaches Expect from Parents.
   - Concerns expressed directly to the coach.
   - Notification of any schedule conflict well in advance.
   - Specific concern in regard to a coach's philosophy and/or expectations.

3. Appropriate Concerns to Discuss with Coaches.
   - The treatment of your child mentally and physically.
   - Ways to help your child improve.
   - Concerns about your child's behavior.

4. Issues Not Appropriate to Discuss with Coaches.
   - Playing time.
   - Team strategy.
   - Play calling.
   - Other student athletes.

5. The Procedure You Should Follow if You Have a Concern to Discuss with a Coach.
   - Call to set up an appointment.
   - If the coach cannot be reached, call the Athletic Director. He will set up a meeting for you.
   - Please do not attempt to confront a coach before or after a contest or practice. These can be emotional times for

both the parent and the coach. Meetings of this nature usually do not promote resolution.

6. What Can a Parent Do if the Meeting With the Coach Did Not Provide a Satisfactory Resolution.
   - Call and set up an appointment with the Athletic Director to discuss the situation.
   - At this meeting the appropriate next step can be determined.

The communication is concluded with the following statement:

> Since research indicates a student involved in co-curricular activities has a greater chance of success during adulthood, these programs have been established. Many of the character traits required to be successful participants are exactly those that will promote a successful life after high school. We hope the information provided within this pamphlet makes both your child's and your experience with the High School Athletic Program less stressful and more enjoyable.

In closing this chapter, the Coaches Code of Ethics of the National Federation Interscholastic Coaches Association is presented to reflect the qualities of leadership that organization expects of interscholastic coaches. (See Figure 3.)

# COACHES
# CODE OF ETHICS
NATIONAL FEDERATION INTERSCHOLASTIC COACHES ASSOCIATION

The function of a coach is to educate students through participation in interscholastic competition. An interscholastic program should be designed to enhance academic achievement and should never interfere with opportunities for academic success. Each student-athlete should be treated as though he or she were the coaches' own, and his or her welfare should be uppermost at all times. Accordingly, the following guidelines for coaches have been adopted by the NFICA Board of Directors.

The **coach** shall be aware that he or she has a tremendous influence, for either good or ill, on the education of the student athlete and, thud, shall never place the value is winning above the value of instilling the highest ideals of character.

The **coach** shall uphold the honor and dignity of the profession. In all personal contact with student-athletes, officials, athletic directors, school administrators, the state high school athletic association, the media, and the public, the coach shall strive to set an example of the highest ethical and moral conduct.

The **coach** shall take an active role in the prevention of drug, alcohol and tobacco abuse.

The **coach** shall avoid the use of alcohol and tobacco products when in contact with players.

The **coach** shall promote the entire interscholastic program of the school and direct his or her program in harmony with the total school program.

The **coach** shall master the contest rules and shall teach them to his or her team members. The coach shall not seek an advantage by circumvention of the spirit or letter of the rules.

The **coach** shall exert his or her influence to enhance sportsmanship by spectators, both directly and by working closely with cheerleaders, pep club sponsors, booster clubs, and administrators.

The **coach** shall respect and support contest officials. The coach shall not indulge in conduct which would incite players or spectators against the officials. Public criticism of officials or players is unethical.

**Before and after contests**, coaches for the competing teams should meet and exchange cordial greetings to set the correct tone for the event.

**A coach** shall not exert pressure on faculty members to give student-athletes special consideration.

**A coach** shall not scout opponents by any means other than those adopted by the league and/or state high school athletic association.

**Figure 3.** NFICA Coaches Code of Ethics

*Chapter 5*

# ORGANIZATION AND ADMINISTRATION OF INTERSCHOLASTIC ATHLETICS

Organization is generally concerned with arranging a group of parts which may be dependent on one another into one whole. In this case, organization provides the machinery which makes an interscholastic athletic program function. Administration is related to the process of adequately conducting the program after it has been organized.

Because of the many factors which influence interscholastic athletics, no one organizational plan can be recommended for all situations. In organizing the program, such considerations as personnel, facilities, and school enrollment will determine to a large extend the type of organization that is best adapted to the circumstances. There are, therefore, many plans and combinations of plans for the organization and administration of interscholastic athletics. In this regard it should be understood that the types of organizational plans and administrative procedures discussed here are merely examples of some of the types found in operation in current interscholastic programs. Thus, this chapter will address such factors as organization at the state and local community level along with several administrative practices and procedures that are important to the success of an interscholastic athletic program.

## ORGANIZATION AT THE STATE LEVEL

State services in interscholastic athletics are characterized by their variety, with each state employing numerous ways of rendering such services. The following are some methods which are used by some states with varying degrees of frequency. That is, not all states use all of these methods but some use many of them.

1. Group conferences and workshops.
2. Conventions
3. Circular letters
4. Local surveys

In addition to these methods some states cooperate closely with the teacher preparation institutions by setting standards through certification requirements and by using the personnel of these institutions as consultants.

Perhaps the most important functions of the state are to devise rules and regulations for the protection of student athletes of the member schools. This is accomplished in part by such procedures as limiting the number of contests, establishing age limits and other eligibility requirements for participants, providing insurance and benefit plans, approving athletic officials, along with a host of other concerns. In some cases member school establishes procedures which are specific to that particular school system. However, all member schools are ordinarily required to abide by the rules established by the state. (See Figure 4 for State of Maryland organization chart).

# MARYLAND PUBLIC SECONDARY SCHOOLS ATHLETIC ASSOCIATION

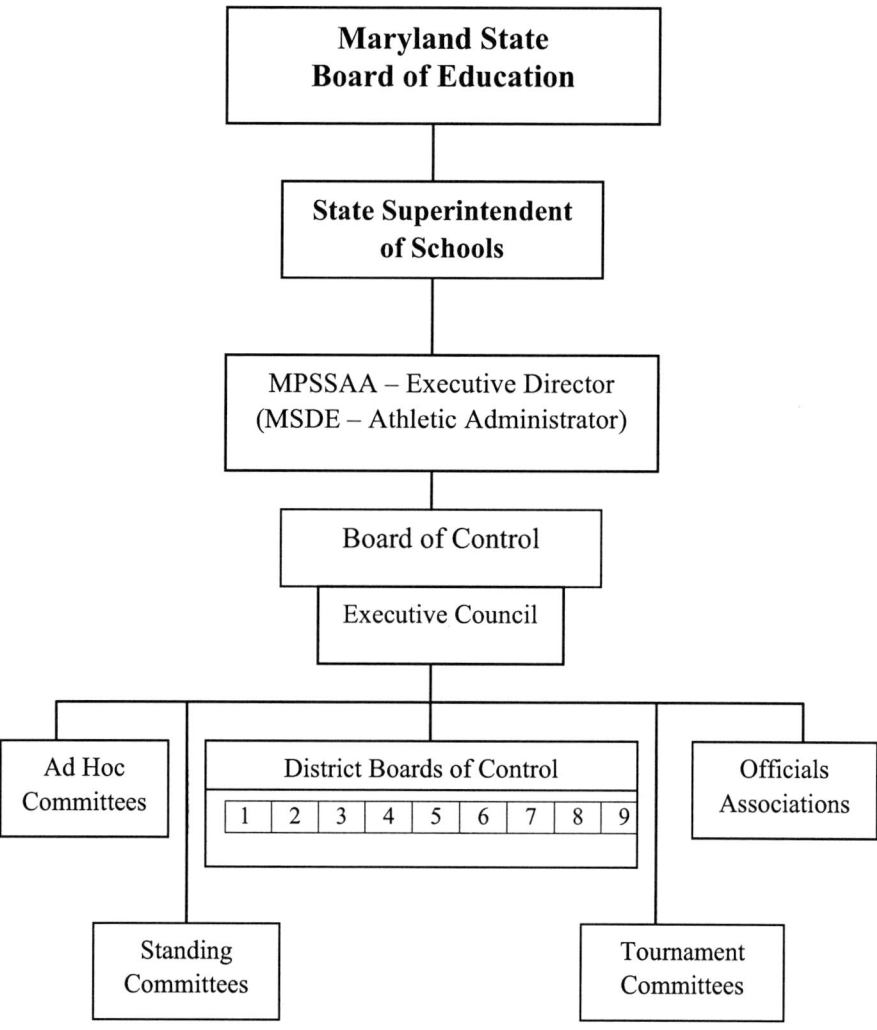

**Figure 4.** State of Maryland Organization Chart

## ORGANIZATION AT THE LOCAL COMMUNITY LEVEL

In considering the organization of interscholastic athletics at the local community level it is perhaps advisable to take into account the organization of grades at the secondary school level.

Traditionally, the three most popular plans of organization among secondary schools are (1) the four-year high school which includes grades nine through twelve, (2) the six-year secondary school which combines the junior and senior high with grades seven through twelve, and (3) the 6-3-3 plan which establishes the junior year high school and the senior high school as separate units.

A common type of division considers the grades of seven, eight, and nine to comprise the junior high school, with grades ten, eleven, and twelve comprising the senior high school.

Another level of organization introduced in recent years in many school systems is designated as the *middle school*. This can comprise ranges of grades from five through eight or six through eight. This form of organization has met with various degrees of success with some educators having a positive attitude toward it and others being opposed to it. However, as a matter of fact, this type of organization was the most prevalent in my surveys. In 70 percent of the cases athletic directors were from schools with grades 9-12; 22 percent from schools with grades 7-12 with the remaining eight percent having other forms of organization.

The type of athletic organization at the local community level will depend upon the size of the community, school population, and the number of schools in the community sponsoring interscholastic athletic teams. In very small communities the superintendent may be the direct supervisor of the athletic program. In other communities this responsibility may be delegated to the school principal. In this regard, it may be said that the principal should assume the same responsibility for interscholastic athletics as he or she does for all other aspects of the educational program in his or her school.

While the final responsibility will fall to the superintendent of schools, in many instances supervisory aspects of athletics will be delegated to other school personnel. For example, a faculty athletic manager, athletic director, coach, or supervisor of physical education may have major charge of the athletic program.

I should mention that some schools do not rely upon an athletic administrator as such, preferring to place the responsibility with an athletic council or committee. This group usually consists of the principal as chairman, with a faculty member serving as treasurer, and the remainder of the committee made up of head coaches of the various varsity sports.

This approach is similar to a management style in business and industry that emphasizes the "team system" which is designed to minimize the traditional concept of *bosses*. While such an approach displaces bosses as such, it does not eliminate the need for leaders.

In any case the present trend according to my surveys is to designate the position of athletic director in secondary schools with an enrollment of 500 or more students.

## ADMINISTRATIVE PRACTICES AND PROCEDURES

The average person who attends a secondary school athletic contest sees only the game and he or she has little realization of the planning that has gone into it before the game actually starts. And such pre-game planning is only a very small fraction of the numerous facets and ramifications that are encountered in the administration of a successful interscholastic athletic program.

There is a tremendous scope of administrative responsibilities connected with the management of such program. Each school is perhaps likely to be unique to the extent that certain administrative concerns manifest themselves in a way peculiar to a specific situation. For this reason there is not likely to be a standardized method of solving all administrative problems. However, there are a number of administrative responsibilities which are common to many schools.

The discussions of certain administrative concerns that follow are based essentially on the findings of my national surveys of secondary school athletic directors.

## Safeguarding Health Participants

There are a number of considerations involving the health and welfare of participants that need to be taken into account. Some of these concerns are discussed here.

*Physical Examinations of Participants*

In my study about two-thirds of the athletic directors said it was their responsibility to "make for the physical examination for each candidate for each athletic activity," and they considered it to be a duty of *extreme* importance. In addition, slightly more than 90 percent "keep a file of physical examination results for students who participate in the interscholastic athletic program." Again, they considered this to be of *extreme* importance.

There are various ways of conducting physical examinations. In many cases the school physician or nurse will handle this task. In others a local physician may be called upon to do this. In fact, 70 percent of the athletic directors "develop a plan for professional personnel such as physicians in the school athletic program."

In my own personal experience some years ago it was not uncommon for the school nurse to disqualify a student because of an elevated heart rate. In many cases this was due to what is now known as "white coat syndrome." In these situations parents had the option of having their own private physician examine the student. And in a majority of cases under a less emotionally-charged environment, the student had a normal heart rate and was allowed to participate.

*Supervision of Facilities*

In my study almost 90 percent of athletic directors "supervised sanitary conditions of athletic facilities." And all athletic directors "coordinated the inspection of all athletic facilities and equipment which may be used to insure safety of spectators and contestants."

*Care and Prevention of Athletic Injuries*

As a preventive measure 98 percent of the athletic directors "arrange for police, ambulance, and other safety departments to have representatives at home athletic contests, if necessary."

Practically all schools require some sort of accident insurance program for student athletes and there are a variety of practices in this regard. Almost two-thirds of the athletic directors in my study were responsible for the development of such a plan. Numerous insurance plans are not available for participants. In some cases commercial insurance companies provide coverage for interscholastic athletes. In some states athletic insurance coverage is provided by the State Athletic Association for member schools. In other instances the local school may have its own plan for protecting participating students.

With regard to athletic injuries and accidents there arises the question of liability. There is always the chance for personnel to be held legally responsible for injuries to participants. Each individual should determine the law concerning injury through negligence in his or her own state and school system.

In general, coaches and athletic directors are not liable, if they can prove they were not negligent. Negligence is commonly determined as the failure to act as a reasonably prudent and careful person would act. In some instances, it may be determined that failure to act at all was negligence.

It is important to note that those individuals with special skills are expected to act at a higher level of prudence than a layman with no special knowledge. Thus, a lifeguard could be held for greater responsibility than another person without a life saving certificates. A coach would be expected to have more knowledge than others about the danger of certain vigorous activities and the use of certain equipment or apparatus.

An athletic director or coach who allows students to use equipment without supervision might be vulnerable if a participant were injured while using the equipment. Signs or posters of warning of the danger or forbidding use of areas or equipment do not necessarily relieve one of his or her responsibility. However, the participant is expected to carry some responsibility for his or her actions. If contributory negligence is proved, that is, with both parties at fault, the responsibility of the coach or athletic director is at least reduced. The student, too, is held for reasonably prudent action for a person of his or her age and experience. Regardless of legal responsibility, the greater moral responsibility for the protection of participants should motivate the athletic director to provide safe areas, equipment and activities. (Of course, there is insurance available for school personnel as well as for student athletic participants.)

Incidentally, over the years as an *expert witness* on the subject I have discerned an increase in the number of lawsuits being brought against school physical education and athletic personnel. However, in most instances these cases have been settled out of court due to insufficient evidence.

Another aspect of care and prevention of injuries is the certification of coaches qualifying them to attend to such injuries. Almost three-fourths of the athletic directors in my study "coordinate a care and prevention of athletic injuries course for coaches and certify course completion." (See Figure 5 for course completion certificate in Washington County, Maryland). The in-service courses are designed essentially for school athletic personnel who have not had professional preparation in the areas of first aid and athletic training.

And finally, another important concern in health of participants in terms of prevention is the "organization and administration of athletic team substance abuse and prevention." More than three-fourths of the athletic directors in my study performed this task.

## Awards

It is customary for schools to recognize student athletes for their achievements, and in my study almost 90 percent of the athletic directors "develop a plan for athletic awards." These awards are usually in the form of the school insignia or initial. While awards criteria may differ from one school to another, each school must conform to guidelines established by the state athletic association. Ordinarily, when awards are given by an outside organization they need to be approved by the local superintendent of schools as well as the state athletic association.

**Figure 5.** Certificate for Care and Prevention of Athletic Injuries for Washington County, Maryland

## Eligibility

In general, interscholastic athletic eligibility is concerned with (1) age limitations, (2) academic performance, (3) student conduct, and (4) attendance.

Although there is some variation among schools regarding *age limitations*, in most case students are ineligible for participation when they reach the age of 10 or 20. More than 80 percent of the athletic directors in my study indicated that they "keep a record of proof of age of each candidate for each athletic activity," a duty they considered to be of *extreme importance*.

As in the case of age limitations the standards of *academic performance* also vary; however, most schools require that a student be passing a certain number of subjects in order to be eligible for participation. Incidentally, there is a segment of the population, albeit minuscule, that subscribes to the notion that there should be no academic requirements for participation in interscholastic athletics. They believe that if there is compulsory education until the age of 16, then students should benefit from any school program regardless of academic standing. It is suggested also that if a boy or girl fails to "make" an interscholastic athletic team that individual is not disqualified from attending a given academic class. With present trends being what they are, it appears that it is completely outside the realm of possibility that such a philosophy will ever be implemented.

Most schools have some sort of *conduct code* that students must abide by if they expect to participate in extracurricular activities, including interscholastic athletics. Depending upon the seriousness of the violation, penalties can range from one contest to expulsion.

As in the case of other eligibility regulations, *attendance* may vary from school system to school system. In general, it is expected that students be enrolled in school for a certain number of classes-usually a minimum of four. I made a study of 43 state activity associations and found that about six percent of them required that students attend only one class to be eligible to participate. I also found that in about one-third of the cases students who had home-based instruction were allowed to participate provided they met certain standards. Among such standards were the following: (1) the student must meet other school eligibility requirements, (2) some schools require that students maintain a certain standardized test score, and (3) the equivalent home program needed approval of the local commissioner of education or state superintendent of schools.

In concluding this section of the chapter it is worth repeating that well over 90 percent of athletic directors performed the duties of "verifying and eligibility of each athlete," and "monitoring and reporting academic ineligibility of athletes."

## Financing the Program

In my study about 60 percent of the athletic directors identified "finances" as the most serious problem in administering an interscholastic athletic program. They cited such factors as "rising costs without rising income," and "difficulty encountered in raising funds." It is not wonder, then, that many of the most important duties that they performed were concerned with financing the program. The following discussions will take into account some of the sources of funding.

*School Budget Allowance*
Most schools receive a specified amount from school allocation of funds, and this, of course, is in the form of "tax dollars." They are very few instances in which this alone finances the entire program, with most athletic directors indicating that this source provides about half of the funding needed. In some cases it provided only 20 percent to less than 50 percent of what athletic directors considered they needed to finance a successful program.

*Gate Receipts*
Prices of admission to athletic contests vary among schools. Gate receipts and season ticket sales were the most satisfactory source of funding for almost one-half of the schools in the survey.

*Fund Raising Events*
Some athletic directors reported that various fund raising events provided up to 75 percent of the funds needed.

Fund raising included all manner of events from "bake sales" to "bull roasts," and all sorts of ingenious methods in between. Some of these included profit from vending machines, parking fees, golf tournaments, program advertising, concessions at athletic events and public solicitations. As far as the latter is concerned, some schools place restrictions on "door-to-door" solicitation by students by limiting the number of these in a school year and confining the solicitations to immediate areas of a given school. One of the reasons given for this is that it could cause poor public relations between the school and community if done on a wide-spread basis.

*Student Athletic Fees*

Less than ten percent of the schools surveyed used an athletic participation fee as a source of funding. A few schools charge a fee for the year and others at the start of each sports season. Amount of the fees vary and usually range from $40.00 to $60.00. I surveyed a number of parents on this issue and found that only about ten percent supported such a plan. In general, it was their feeling that students should not have "to pay to play."

*Donations*

About one-fourth of the schools in my survey relied on donations as a means of funding, and in about half of these cases the donations came from an athletic "booster club."

One form of donation that is growing in popularity as a means of funding interscholastic athletic programs is *corporate sponsorship*. This has long been an excellent supplementary source of funding for some colleges, and it is not uncommon for large corporations to donate hundreds of thousands of dollars to have their logo on a scoreboard or basketball court. Although it has not reached such proportions at the secondary school level, many schools and state athletic associations are exploring this possibility as a lucrative source of funding.

As secondary school personnel examine the area of corporate sponsorship it is important to think in terms of useful guidelines for this purpose. In this regard, John Tarman[1], Director of Marketing for the California Interscholastic Federation has developed what he terms "Seven Steps to Sponsorship Success." These steps are identified in the following discussion along with some highlights under each step.

1. Establish Goals
   - ❖ Short Term vs. Long Term Goals
     - How Much Revenue is Needed?
     - What/Who Are Available Resources
   - ❖ 3 Year Plan
     - Write a Marketing Plan: Ask an Association Officer and/or Your Executive Committee to Review and Approve Your Plan to Ensure That it is Consistent with Your State Philosophy & Policies

2. Identify Your Audience and Your Market
   - What Types of Business Will Most Benefit from Sponsoring Your State Championship Events and Programs?
   - Primary Target Audience
   - Match Your Primary Target Audience with that of Potential Sponsors

3. Create an Inventory of Sponsorship Products
   - ❖ Identify Those Events/Programs Which Involve a Captured Target Audience
   - ❖ Sample Sponsorship Products
     - Award/Recognition Sponsorships
     - Year Round Championship Event Sponsorships
     - Sport Specific Sponsorships

---

[1] Tarman, John, Seven steps to sponsorship success, Paper presented at the meeting of the National Federation of State High School Associations, July 16, 1996, Tarpon Springs, Florida.

4. Identify Specific Features and Corresponding Benefits Appropriate for Each Level/Type of Sponsorship
   ❖ Tangible vs. Intangible Benefits
     • Create Features Which Will Provide Tangible Benefits to Your Sponsor
   ❖ Tailor Features/Benefits to Satisfy Specific Advertising/Promotional Needs of Your Prospective Sponsors
   ❖ Remember –You are Recommending That a Corporate Sponsor Make a Marketing Investment in Your Program: Ensure That the Sponsor's Return on the Investment is as Quantifiable as Possible
   ❖ Price Each Sponsorship Product
     • Determine Price by Assigning Value for Each Feature
   ❖ Establish a Menu of Sponsorship Packages
     • Be Sure That no Two Sponsorship Packages Are Exactly Alike in Features
     • Offer a Variety of Products With Different Price Points

5. Create Sales Tools for Use During Presentations to Corporate Decision Makers
   ❖ Most People Process Information Best When it is Presented Visually
   ❖ Quantify as Many Facts, Features & Benefits as Possible
   ❖ Whenever Possible, Use Third Party Testimony
     • Generate a List of State Association Sponsors Who Are Satisfied Sponsors and Will Enthusiastically Endorse Your Sponsorship Program

6. Presentations to Corporate Decision Makers
   ❖ Initial Contact
     • Phone Contact
     • Identify the Decision Maker Within the Corporation
     • Goal-Get an Appointment for a Meeting in Person
   ❖ Personal Presentation
     • Before you Present Your Program, Ask Questions About Corporation's Business and Promotional Needs

- The Purpose of These "Probing" Questions are twofold:
  → To Generate Active Conversational Participation From Client
  → To Solicit Information Regarding Merchant Needs, Current Advertising & Promotional Investments, Target Market...etc. in Order to Better Position the Features and Benefits of Your Sponsorship Program
- ❖ Probing Questions (Sample List)
  - "What is your target market?"
  - "What % of your market do high school students represent?"
  - "Are you doing any specific advertising/promotions in order to increase your high school student business?"
  - "What % of your current business do families of high school students represent?"
- ❖ Present Your Program
  - Briefly Describe Your State Association Service to Its Member Schools
  - Present Sponsorship Features & Benefits-Emphasizing Those Which You Believe Will Best Satisfy Your Client's Needs
  - Listen and Respond (using sales tools) to Any Concerns/Objections
- ❖ Ask for the Order
  - Trial Close
    → "Do you think that you might benefit most from year-around program sponsorship or an individual event sponsorship?"

7. Fostering Relationships With Sponsors
   - ❖ Goal-To Build Long-term Relationships With Sponsors
     - Creating a Sense of Investment/Ownership is Your Paramount Goal
   - ❖ Schedule an Annual End-of-the-Year Meeting With Current Sponsors to Evaluate Features and Benefits
     - Always Ask About Changes in Sponsor's Needs

- Encourage Personal Involvement by Sponsors
- Creative Environments for Personal Networking by Inviting Sponsors to Various Functions (i.e. athletic banquets, assemblies, etc…)
- Insure Personal Recognition at Appropriate Gatherings/Events
- Always Ask Sponsors for Referrals

In times past corporate sponsorships were viewed more or less as a goodwill endeavor with little regard for a profitable return. In more modern times, however, corporations are likely to look for what they can expect from their investment. For this reason beneficiaries may be expected to indicate what they might provide in return for financial considerations. A specific case in point is that of the Pennsylvania Interscholastic Athletic Association when it considered sponsors for support of its 4$^{th}$ annual PIAA Officials' Convention and 35 Year Recognition Banquet. Dr. Robert A. Lombardi, PIAA Associate Executive Director has provided the following:

"In return for financial considerations, PIAA will minimally:"

1. Place name in the registration packet of every convention attendee.
2. Place logo/name on the convention schedule.
3. Place name in the banquet program.
4. Announcement at the banquet and recognizing corporate support.
5. Publicly recognize involvement with PIAA with press releases.
6. Hang corporate banner in the registration area of PIAA Officials' Convention.
7. Meet the PIAA Staff.
8. Provide the opportunity to attend the executive Director's reception.
9. Provide opportunity to play in Officials' Golf Tournament.
10. Provide the opportunity to attend the PIAA Officials' Convention Banquet.
11. Provide a photo session citing your support of the PIAA Officials' Convention for distribution in local and statewide media.

12. Provide name to all 490 PIAA Officials' Chapters statewide for their information to support your organization.
13. Provide name to all 15, 299 registered officials statewide through Officials' Newsletter.
14. PIAA token of appreciation.

"Other considerations may be possible through negotiation and the type of corporate involvement desired."

Any discussion of corporate sponsorship should consider the general question of the relationship of a school athletic department with any commercial organization. While the nature of any contact with local commercial organization may vary, it is essential that a cooperative relationship be established between commercial groups and the school department of athletics.

It is highly important that requests from commercial organizations be evaluated with respect to the manner in which they may ultimately benefit the students. When commercial groups in the community request the cooperation of the school in sponsoring an activity, the motives for sponsorship should be explored. If it can be shown that the best interests and welfare of the children and youth of the community are paramount, the school is not only justified by perhaps obligated to render wholehearted cooperation. This is particularly true when the activity in question is within the realm of the athletic objectives of the school. On the other hand, if a commercial organization wishes to sponsor an activity for purposes of self-gain and propaganda, students should certainly not be used as the medium for such exploitation. When the athletic director acts in the capacity of an agent for the school athletic department, it is evident that he or she must use tact and discretion in evaluating requests and recommendations made by commercial organizations. This is imperative so that the school will not fall victim to undesirable public relations.

Another factor sometimes concerned with wholesome relationships with community commercial organizations pertain to the purchase of athletic equipment and supplies. In this regard, local dealers should be taken into consideration when the procurement of new equipment and supplies is contemplated. If it is the responsibility of the athletic director to recommend school needs with respect to equipment and supplies, it may desirable for him or her to make these needs known to local dealers. If they can meet the needs as specified, they should be given every opportunity to do so. While the efficacy and diplomacy of this plan is readily apparent, there have been cases where schools have gained the enmity of local commercial organizations by failing to follow this procedure.

In summary, I should mention again that this chapter has dealt only with those organizational and administrative concerns that participant in my study found to be most prevalent. There are many other situations that conform athletic directors as seen in the various duties performed by them and reported in Chapter 3.

*Chapter 6*

# SCHEDULING FOR ATHLETIC COMPETITION

The athletic director is often required to prepare schedules for athletic events, and this activity provides any number of problems. Thus, there are certain basic factors that need to be taken into account in the preparation of schedules,

In planning the competition for athletic events the director must keep one thought constantly in mind. In keeping with available facilities, time allotted, and the number of participants a type of competition should be selected that will insure sufficient playing time. If scheduling of athletic events is completely new to the director he or she should obtain entries early in order to determine the number of teams or individual contestants. One more major factor must be taken into consideration. For activities in most climates the weather must be taken into account when the schedule is prepared. A schedule that would finish the last day of school might not be completed because there are usually some days, particularly in the spring season when activities may have to be curtailed because of inclement weather.

## SINGLE ELIMINATION TOURNAMENT

The single elimination tournament is one of the quickest ways of determining a champion. The term *single elimination* indicates that little participation is involved for at least half of the teams or contestants. There are values in this type of tournament, however, and it may be the only possible method by which the competition can be arranged.

When the director plans any kind of tournament he or she must know how many contests will be necessary to complete the competition. In the single elimination tournament there will always be one less contest than the number of teams. For example, if there are eight teams entered in a single elimination tournament, there will be a total of seven games. Figure 6. shows an example of an eight-team single elimination tournament.

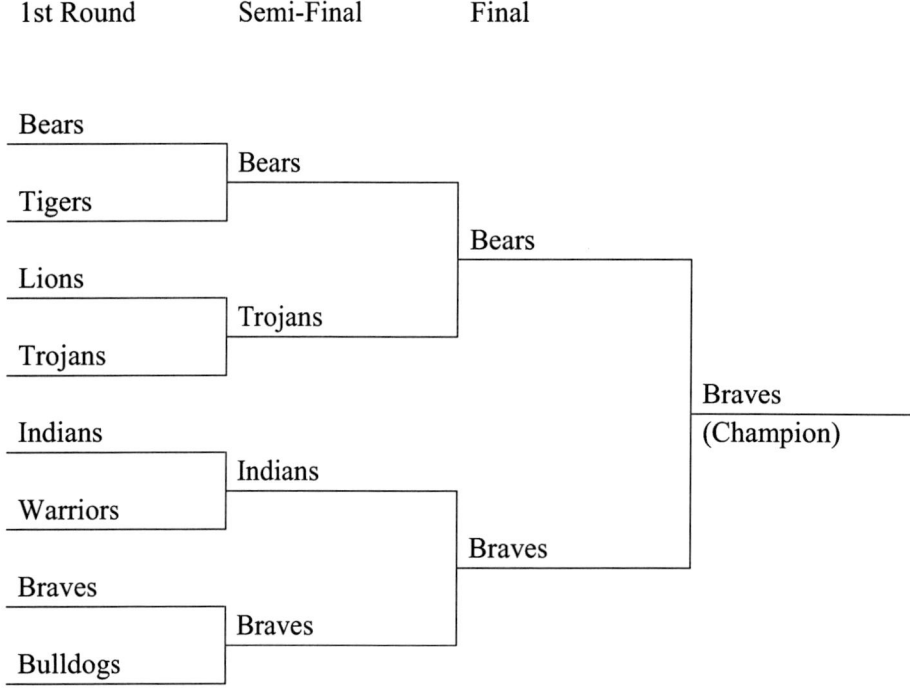

**Figure 6.** Single Elimination Tournament for Eight Teams

There is a bracket for each game and the brackets should be even in numbers. It is not necessary that there be a team for each line but the number of lines should equal a perfect power of two, such as 4, 8, 16, 32, 64, and 128. If the number of teams does not equal one of these figures the *bye rule* is used. This means that the number of teams should be subtracted from the next highest power of two. For example, if there are six teams in a single elimination tournament, six would be subtracted from the next highest power of two. This means that six would be subtracted from eight. The difference is two and this means that there would be two byes. It is necessary to complete all byes in the first round of a tournament. Figure 7. shows an example illustrating this point.

If the director has some idea of the ability of the participants they may be "seeded" in the tournament. This procedure places the best participant at the opposite ends of the draw where they will not meet until the semi-finals or finals. It may not be fair to seed terms or individuals if points are given for all-year trophies because it automatically removes the chance of the better teams or players from meeting, while the weaker teams must always play the stronger teams. Third and fourth places can easily be determined by having the semi-finalists play.

On some occasions the league play is followed by one of the types of elimination tournaments. A director can easily schedule field or courts in advance, even though he or she does not know which teams will be playing. The "draw" or game is scheduled rather than the teams. In this way, he or she does not have to wait until the leagues are finished to reserve the necessary space and time.

If there are two leagues approaching the final playoffs, the director can schedule the games as follows:

**Figure 7.** Single Elimination Tournament for Six Teams

## Schedule

*Tuesday----4:30*

Court 1-----A1

Court 2-----A2

*Wednesday--4:30*

Court 1-----B1

Court 2-----B2

*Thursday---4:30*

Court 1-----A3

Court 2-----B3

*Friday---4:30*

Court 1-----Championship

## CONSOLATION TOURNAMENT

This kind of tournament provides more participation than the single eliminating insuring that each entry plays at least two times. Only the first round losers go back into the playback or consolation rounds. Figure 8. shows the champion and consolation winner for a draw of eight. Figure 9 shows the same for a draw of seven.

Seeding and byes are treated in the same manner as in single elimination contests. In the case of byes, the team that loses the first contest played in any round goes into the consolation tournament. If, in Figure 8. the Braves had lost to the Warriors, the Braves would have gone back into the consolation round, as it was their first loss.

## DOUBLE ELIMINATION TOURNAMENT

As the name implies this type of tournament assures that a team will participate until it has lost twice.

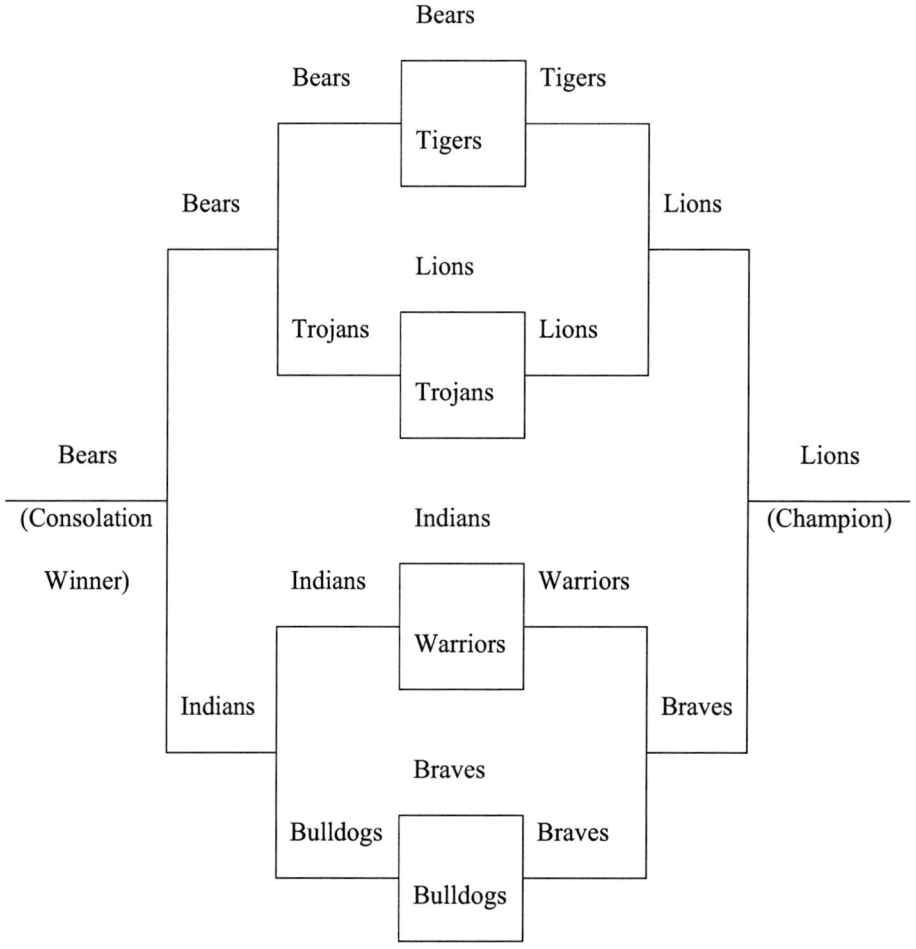

**Figure 8.** Consolation Tournament for Eight Teams

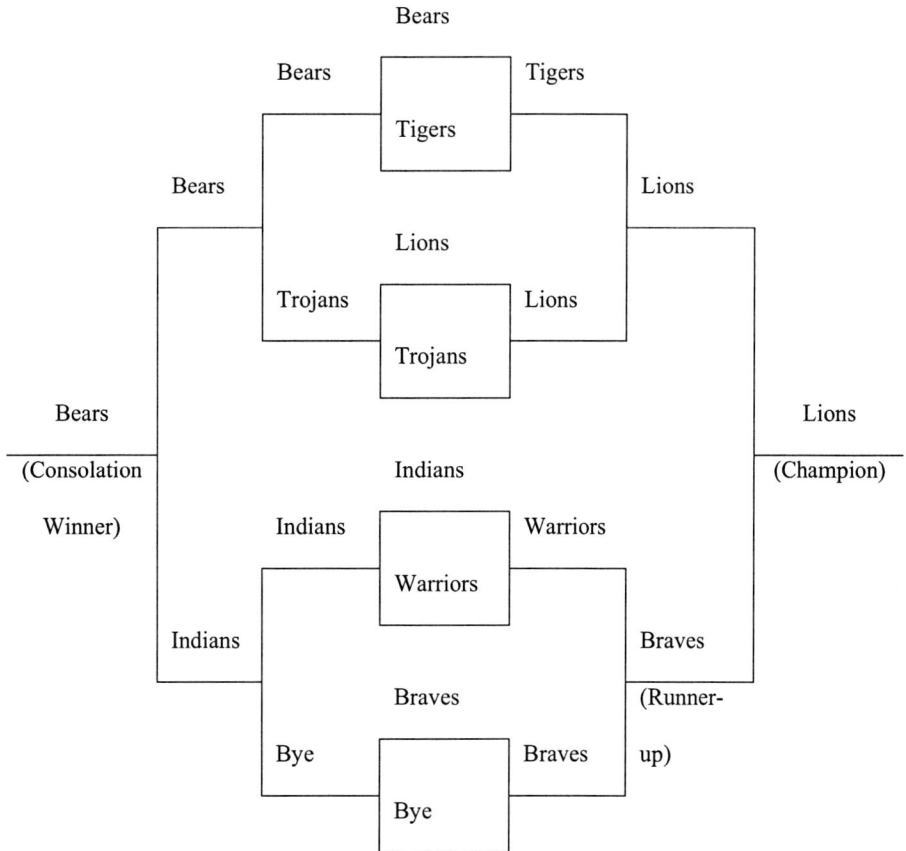

**Figure 9.** Consolation Tournament for Seven Teams

The draw is similar to the consolation tournament in that the losers go to the left and the winners to the right. Cross bracketing reduces the chances of two teams playing each other more than once. To determine the champion the winner on the left plays the winner on the right. However, the winner on the left must win two games from the winner on the right because the team on the left has already lost one game. Figure 10. shows an example of this type of tournament.

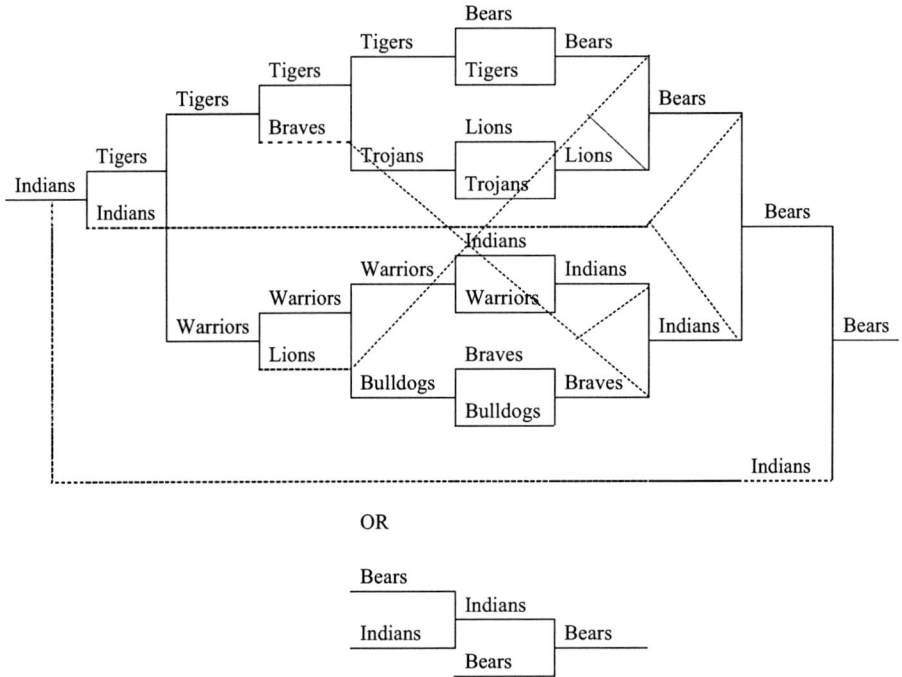

**Figure 10.** Double Elimination Tournament for Eight Teams

Another method of conducting a double elimination tournament is to make a complete new draw among the losers. The team that have lost twice are dropped, and the teams that have lost once are redrawn with the undefeated teams.

Byes and seeding are handled in the same manner as in the single elimination tournament. In double elimination tournaments there will be one or two less games than twice the number of teams. Consequently, in the example in Figure 10. there will be 14 or 15 games depending upon whether the winner on the right loses one game or none.

A double elimination tournament composed of a draw not a perfect power of two is structurally the same. The byes are merely carried through as you would a losing team from the first round. See Figure 11.

## FLIGHTS AND QUALIFYING ROUNDS

Qualifying rounds should be used for the purpose of separating the players or teams into various flights for further play. It does not seem justifiable to have qualification requirements for contests if the players who fail to qualify for further competition are eliminated. This procedure limits their participation to one effort.

In qualifying events that have numerical scores a specified score can be listed as the lowest qualifying score, or a certain number of qualifiers can be designated, such as the highest 10, the second highest 10 and so on.

Another method, illustrated in Figure 12. that can be used for making more equal leagues is a modification of the single elimination tournament. Considerable time is needed and therefore, only a sport conducted during a long season is practicable for use with this procedure. The teams may be placed arbitrarily in brackets and the teams that win two games can be placed in one league (1, 5, 9, 13). The teams that win one and lose one are placed in two other leagues (2, 6, 10, 14) and (3, 7, 11, 15). The teams that lose two are placed in a fourth league (4, 8, 12, 16). These leagues can then compete for four championships determined by round robin play.

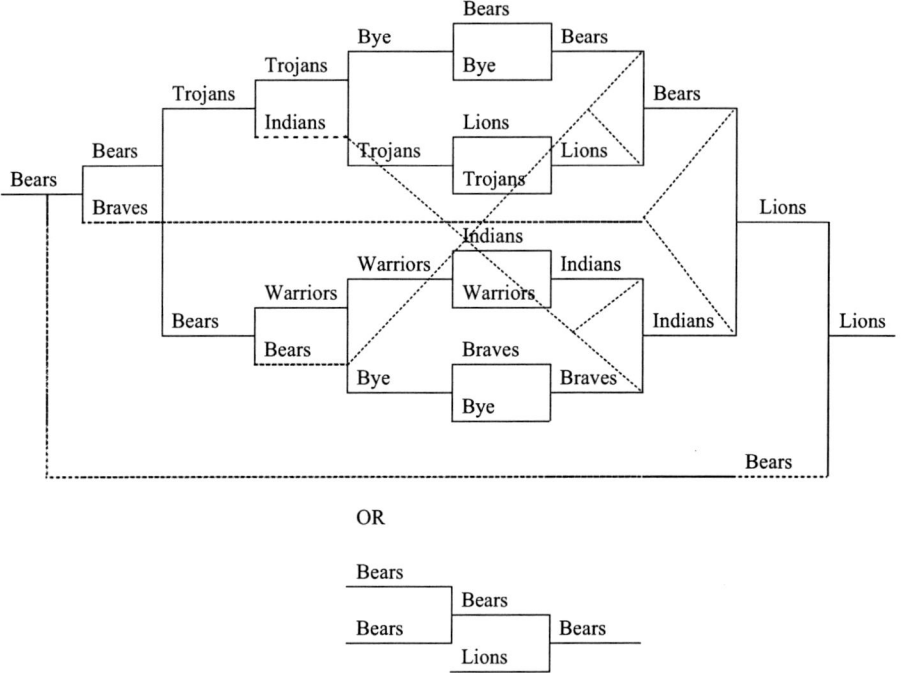

**Figure 11.** Double Elimination Tournament for Six Teams

# Scheduling for Athletic Competition

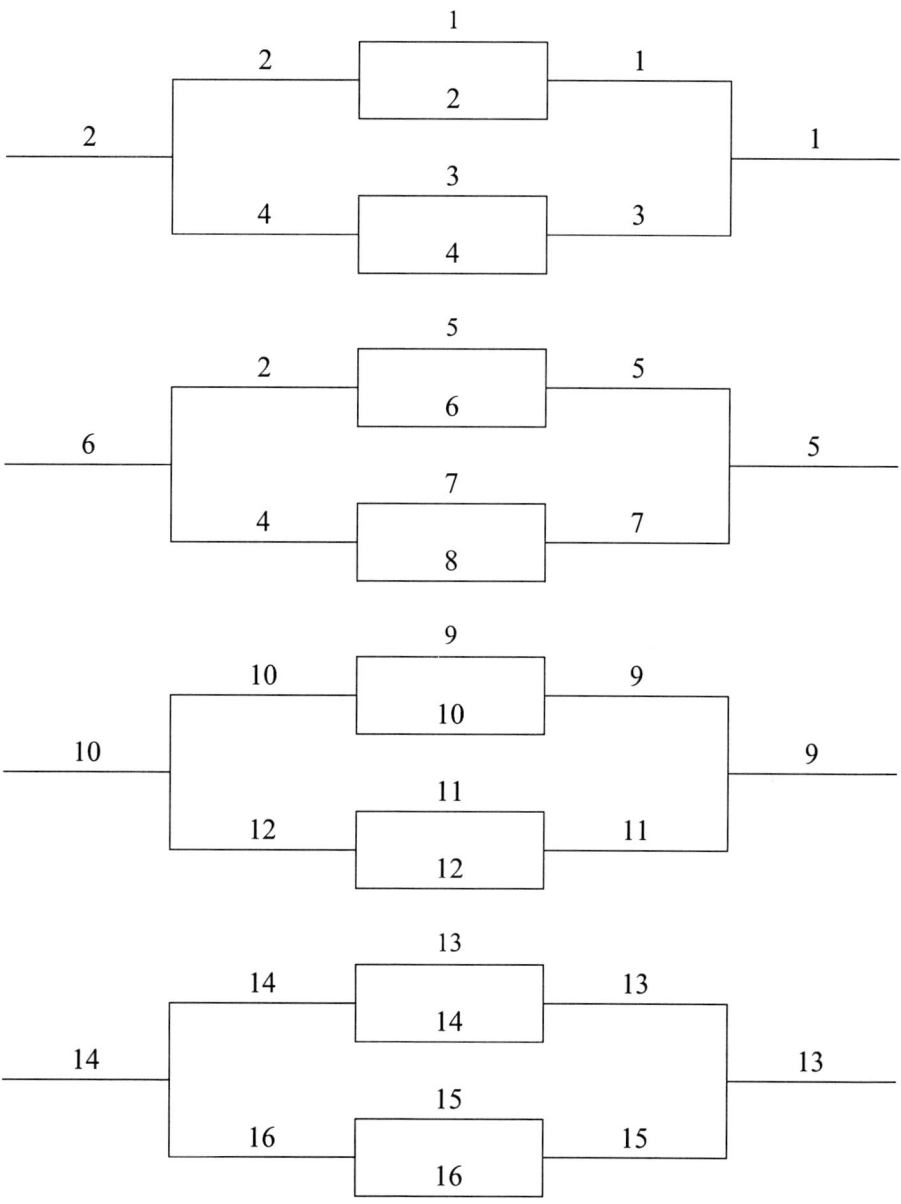

**Figure 12.** Procedure for Placement of Teams in Leagues

## ROUND ROBIN

This type of competition results in a more valid champion because every team has an opportunity to play every other team.

One of the first considerations is round robin play after the teams have been entered is to determine the number of games that will be necessary to complete all of the leagues plus the play-offs. The formula $N(N-1)/2$ will give the number of games in a round robin. N refers to the number of teams entered. For example, if six teams were entered there would be a total of 15 games. This is computed by substituting in the formula as follows:

$6(6-1)/2 = 6(5)/2 = 30/2 = 15.$

Any number of teams may compete on a round robin basis. The example given here is six teams. This means that each team will play five games. The total group of teams can be divided into groups or blocks of six, or nearly six teams. If there are 24 teams there would be four blocks of six teams each. Each block would require 15 games to complete the block, making 60 games for the regular schedule. If two blocks of 12 were used it would take 132 games to complete the regular schedule. This number of games would require many weeks to play. If three blocks of eight were used, there would be three block winners which might make it difficult to arrange the play-offs fairly. With four blocks of six, the four winning teams could easily be drawn for a four-team single elimination tournament.

In drawing up the round robin schedule it is convenient to use the following system:

| 1st round | 2nd round | 3rd round | 4th round | 5th round |
|---|---|---|---|---|
| 1-6 | 1-5 | 1-4 | 1-3 | 1-2 |
| 2-5 | 6-4 | 5-3 | 4-2 | 3-6 |
| 3-4 | 2-3 | 6-2 | 5-6 | 4-5 |

Team names should be substituted for the numbers. It should be noted that the number 1 remains stationary while the rest of the numbers move in a counter-clockwise fashion. Either direction can be used as long as the number 1 remains as a fixed number. If there are an unequal number of teams, such as five, the numbers rotate around *bye*. The bye in this case does not mean that the team has less games to play. It signifies, rather, that the team has an open date.

| 1st round | 2nd round | 3rd round | 4th round | 5th round |
|---|---|---|---|---|
| bye-5 | bye-4 | bye-3 | bye-2 | bye-1 |
| 1-4 | 5-3 | 4-2 | 3-1 | 2-5 |
| 2-3 | 1-2 | 5-1 | 4-5 | 3-4 |

It may not always be possible, because of certain unavoidable circumstances, to play the needed games each day to complete each series. Postponements care possible because it matters little which games are played first.

The block system is a convenient form for scoring purposes because each block can be numbered with a win and loss column adjacent to the team's name. An easily understood record is then available to anyone who wishes to check the standings.

The standings in round robin play are often determined on a percentage basis. This is computed by dividing the number of games won by the number of games played. For example, if a team won six games and lost four out of a total of ten games played, ten would be divided by six giving a percentage of .600.

Another way of determining the standings in round robin play is to award two points for a victory, one point for a tie and no points for a defeat. This method differs from the percentage method in that it gives credit for games that end in a tie.

## SOME IMPORTANT AIDS IN SCHEDULING MAKING

The following suggestions are submitted for the purpose of helping the director quickly determine certain necessary information needed in schedule preparation. N refers to the number of entries.

1. The formula N-1 will determine the number of games necessary to complete a single elimination tournament.
2. The formula N (2) –1 or 2 will determine the number of games necessary to complete a double elimination tournament.
3. The formula N (N-1)/2 will determine the number of games necessary to complete a round robin.
4. The number of byes in a tournament may be determined by subtracting the number of entries from the next highest power of two.

*Chapter 7*

# PUBLIC RELATIONS IN INTERSCHOLASTIC ATHLETICS

The idea of the necessity for good school-community public relations is not new.

However, in recent years rapidly changing patterns in our culture have increased interest and activity. As a consequence, the problem of school-community relationships has become somewhat more complicated than has been the case in the past.

If a community is to be effective in contributing to democratic living, school officials and citizens of the community should perhaps accept the responsibility to integrate the agencies within the community which are related to interscholastic athletics. In other words, all persons involved in any way, either with the school or community agencies, should consider pooling their resources for the best interest and welfare of all of the children and youth within the community.

## SCHOOL AND COMMUNITY RELATIONSHIPS

There are numerous ways in which school and community relationships in certain phases of interscholastic athletics can be affected. In general these might be classified into the following broad categories.

1. Community use of the school athletic facilities

2. School use of community resources
   3. Relationship with cooperating community agencies

## Community Use of School Athletic Facilities

In a large number of cases schools are recognizing the importance of community use of school facilities. This is particularly true in communities where the school offers the most feasible facility for sports and recreation.

The use of school athletic facilities by community groups has tow noteworthy aspects. First, it helps to meet some of the recreational needs of people in the community. Second, members of the community using the facilities are more likely to develop an appreciation of the program in general, and also of the school's needs in interscholastic athletics. As a consequence, the school's requests for improved or new facilities is likely to receive more wide-spread attention.

## School Use of Community Resources

It could serve a useful purpose for the athletic director to explore all existing community resources in order to provide for the best possible program. When good school and community relationships exist this becomes a relatively easy procedure. Consequently, when there is community use of the school athletic facilities, a reciprocal arrangement can be established.

Frequently there may be recreational facilities in the community which are idle during school hours. When these facilities are near the school the athletic director may wish to investigate their possible use for the school program. For example, a nearby community center or Y. M. C. A. may have a swimming facility which can be used by the school at certain periods during the day. Likewise, municipal outdoor areas in the form of play fields have been used to good advantage for school athletic activities when desirable relationships exist between community and school officials.

## Relationships with Cooperating Community Agencies

While the greatest responsibility for the growth and development of students rests with the schools, there are many other public and private agencies which are in a position to accept some of this responsibility. Some of these agencies include among others, Girl Scouts, Boy Scouts, community centers, church organizations, service clubs, fraternal groups, Young Men's and Young Women's Christian Associations, and numerous municipal organizations.

In order to avoid unnecessary duplication and overlapping of the work of the school and outside agencies it is essential that there be some sort of coordination. This is especially true because in the majority of cases the school and outside agencies have much the same objectives in view.

It appears that school officials should assume the leadership necessary in establishing cooperative relationships with the outside agencies. This procedure is recommended since students will be taking part in the school athletic program. In this respect the athletic director seems to be in an ideal position to initiate desirable relationships with other agencies which provide athletic and recreation programs for children and youth. In communities where a good relationship is present it has been found that most of the agencies are willing to cooperate with the athletic director and other school officials to give optimum service to students.

# THE PLACE OF THE ATHLETIC DIRECTOR IN COMMUNITY RELATIONS

Acceptance of school policies by the citizens of the community is essential if the needs of boys and girls are to be met to the fullest extent. A competent athletic director will accept the responsibility for establishing and developing relationships with people in the community so that the end result will be an improved program of interscholastic athletics. There are several ways in which this can be accomplished.

The athletic director should be properly adjusted to the community. Because he or she will be called on many times to perform a variety of community functions, it will be necessary for him or her to establish certain desirable contacts in the best interests of community relations and the welfare of students. This may mean that the athletic director will hold active membership in some of the local organizations, or at least contribute to them in the most desirable way when called upon to do so.

It also seems advisable that the athletic director help coaches make a proper adjustment to the community in order to contribute to greater job satisfaction. In the case of new coaches it may be well for the athletic director to help them find suitable living quarters. Also, he or she can inform new coaches with respect to such community conditions as the socioeconomic level, racial and religious groups, plan of community government, and other factors concerned with the general community social background. Information such as this might well contribute to the difference between success and failure on the new job. In other words, when coaches are properly informed with respect to the community background they may avoid some pitfalls that could be encountered if this knowledge is withheld. The athletic director should also recognize the contributions of coaches to the community, and he or she should make these contributions known through the proper channels.

In addition to the importance of the human relations involving the athletic director and staff in community relationships, there is the necessity for the athletic director to know the community. When he or she has a sufficient knowledge of the community and surrounding area, program planning is facilitated. As a consequence, needs of children and youth in the community are more likely to be met through the school athletic program.

A somewhat thorough knowledge of the community may be obtained through the survey technique. The extent of detail and comprehensiveness of a community survey should be governed by the size of the community. However, in order to receive the benefit of all community resources, some type of survey might well be undertaken by the athletic director, coaches, and students.

The athletic director and other members of the staff should recognize that they are citizens of the community in which they live. As such, it should be expected that they perform those functions required of worthwhile community citizens. In as much as the athletic director and coaches are likely to exert a substantial influence on the future lives of students, it is all the more important that they attempt to set an example with respect to good citizenship.

## Some Community Functions Performed by Secondary School Athletic Directors

The athletic director is usually a respected member of the community. As such, naturally certain functions are either formally or informally designated to him or her. These may include such duties as being a member of the recreation board, and supervising playgrounds. Regardless of the position, his or her functions include keeping the public informed about the activities of the athletic program and promoting a congruous understanding between the public schools and the various groups which make up the population at all levels.

A composite of all community population levels indicates the importance of the duty to "provide a plan for public relations for your department." Similarly, people attest to the difficulty involved in the performance of this function.

The modern concept of public relations goes far beyond publicity, or merely keeping the public informed about the activities of the school. In reality, public relations involves a congruous understanding and relationship between the public schools and the various public groups which make up the population at all levels, local, state, and national.

## ORGANIZING FOR PUBLIC RELATIONS IN INTERSCHOLASTIC ATHLETICS

Although the superintendent of schools may have the ultimate responsibility for public relations for the entire school system, the athletic director is likely to be a key figure with regard to the public relations aspect of his or her department. It may not seem feasible in all cases to have a highly organized leadership in the best interests of the schools in meeting the needs of students through good public relations.

It might be well for the athletic director to convey the idea to staff members that they are all a part of the public relations team. This can be done in part through such techniques as conferences and bulletins. This type of cooperative organization is likely to make staff members feel that they have a definite responsibility as far as public relations of the department are concerned. This plan also presents a more or less protective advantage for all staff members. This is important in those instances where some individuals have fallen victim to unjustified circumstances which may have resulted in poor public relations.

## PRINCIPLES OF PUBLIC RELATIONS

If the athletic director is to assume any part of the responsibility for public relations, it is essential that he or she operate on a basis of sound and valid principles. It might be well to enlist the cooperation of other staff members in selecting these guides to action.

While principles of public relations may be somewhat general in nature, it seems advisable that a set of principles be devised which are peculiar to the field of education. In this connection, the following set of school public relations set forth in the Twenty-Eighth Yearbook of the American Association of School Administrators is worthy of note.

1. *School public relations must be honest in intent and execution.* This is undeniably so, for by the very nature of public relations the character of its effort is on display for critical examination by numerous publics. Any misrepresentation carries not only the burden of its own lost opportunity to inform, but the doubled penalty of eventual public censure and wrath.
2. *School public relations must be intrinsic.* This principle means that the public relations value of the educational program itself is the proper basis for the school public relations effort.
3. *School public relations must be continuous.* A continuing stimulus produces a more highly predictable and stronger response than an intermittent or random stimulus.
4. *School public relations must be positive in approach.* Negative statements should be studiously avoided in dealing with school publics. Denials usually are wasted breath. Statements regarding what the schools are not doing generally are misguided and should always give way to a positive statement of what the schools are doing.
5. *School public relations should be comprehensive.* School public relations should be broad and varied- broad in the sense that no

phase of the school program is ignored and no segment of the staff excluded; varied in that no possible medium of contact with any public shall be missed.

6. *School public relations should be sensitive to its publics.* School public relations should be a two-way process. Too many educators have assumed that the purpose of public relations is "to sell" the public their ideas. They have ignored the attitudes, opinions, drives, and desires of the public itself.

7. *The ideas communicated must be simple.* He who would tell an effective story to his publics must study not only the meaning but the emotional connotation of words. He must be content to use words which mean essentially the same thing to most people. These are the simple words.

Although the above principles are concerned primarily with public relations in the entire school program, they are also applicable in a general way of the interscholastic athletic program. However, it seems advisable also that the athletic director has a working set of principles pointed specifically toward public relations in athletics. The following list represents a tentative set of such principles.

1. The interscholastic program must offer information that is interesting to a given public if it wishes to influence that particular public.
2. Methods useful in influencing a certain public must be done skillfully by the athletic department and/or the department's representatives.
3. Department public relations must be compatible with the school's athletic objectives.
4. Data concerning the interscholastic athletic program should be issued continuously and be characterized by reliability.
5. Faculty members and students should be continuously informed about the objectives of the interscholastic athletic program.
6. Members of the athletic department should participate when feasible in community activities.
7. Public relations should be based on needs and interest of specific publics.

Although these principles pertain specifically to public relations in interscholastic athletics, it should be kept in mind that all of them may not be applicable in all situations. For this reason they should perhaps be used as a rough guide and, the athletic director and coaches should rely chiefly on rules for action which are adaptable at the local community level.

## AGENTS AND MEDIA FOR PUBLIC RELATIONS IN INTERSCHOLASTIC ATHLETICS

In the field of public relations, agents refer to the human element, individual or group, through which aspects of the interscholastic athletic program reach the various publics. Among the most important agents are the students and athletic department staff members. Media are concerned more with the materials or techniques used to establish good public relations. In this regard, I asked several hundred athletic directors to identify the three most important public relations media. The following list shows the percent of time each medium was suggested.

1. Print media such as newspapers (86%)
2. Word of mouth (38%)
3. School promotion programs such as assemblies (36%)
4. Radio broadcasts (34%)
5. Contact with community civic organizations (30%)
6. Cable TV broadcasts (30%)
7. School publications (24%)
8. Booster club activities (24%)
9. Winning programs (22%)
10. Internet website (6%)
11. School TV programs (4%)
12. Public recognition of corporate sponsors (4%)
13. Business contacts (4%)
14. Camps (2%)

With regard to the above list I would like to make specific mention of the internet website as an important medium. As noted, when I did my survey only six percent used this method; however, scores of athletic directors indicated that it is something that they are seriously exploring. To point up its usefulness as a relatively new public relations medium, the following statements by Mark Schlenoff, Athletic Director of the Baltimore, Maryland Polytechnic Institute are very appropriate.

> I don't know what I'd do without the use of the internet in many of my daily tasks as Athletic Director. One important example is the use of the *Weather Channel* during the spring season which informs me what the possibilities of getting games played when a weather front approaches. I've played while others have canceled due to the weather maps available to me. My Principal also asks me to log-on when we have important activities planned so we know whether to have them inside or outside.
>
> Other examples of my use of the internet are:
> - frequent checks of my e-mail
> - check the Maryland Public Secondary School
> - Athletic Association web page where many useful items are located (especially the "open date" page where we share open dates with other schools), updated post-season tournament brackets, useful forms, etc.
> - maintaining our schools web page with notes to parents and alumni, scores and team records, and other interesting items as they arise
> - logging on to discussion pages through my online newsgroup giving me access to ideas with others in coaching, officiating and teaching hints
> - logging on to web pages maintained by coaches of various sports which include tips, open dates, etc.
> - logging on to vendor's web pages and purchasing materials and supplies online
> - logging on to map pages when we need to find locations of schools, fields, etc.

There is little question that "going online" appears to have unlimited potential, not only as a public relations medium, but for many other aspects of interscholastic athletics as well.

In summarizing this chapter, it can be said that in general, the agents provide the impetus for implementation of sound public relations through all of the available valid media in establishing relationships with a variety of publics. The publics may be conveniently classified into the three broad categories of parents, non-parents, and taxpayers. Naturally, there will be a certain amount of overlapping among these broad categories.

It can be readily discerned that public relations becomes a two-way course. For instance, attitudes, opinions, criticisms and suggestions are apt to be reflected by one or more publics with respect to their feelings about the interscholastic athletic program.

*Chapter 8*

# ATHLETIC DIRECTORS UNDER STRESS

In Chapter 3 it was mentioned that considering the innumerable duties the athletic director is called upon to perform and the responsibility he or she must assume, it is a position that could include any number of stress-inducing situations. This became much more definitive for me upon evaluating the responses in my survey regarding the stressors encountered by athletic directors. However, before discussing these causes of stress and ways of coping with them, it seems advisable to go into some detail about the phenomenon of stress. I say this because so many of the athletic directors in my study revealed a lack of knowledge about the subject, and indicated that they would be interested in understanding about the scientific dimensions of stress.

## THE MEANING OF STRESS

There is no solid agreement regarding the derivation of the term *stress*. For example, some sources suggest that the term is derived from the Latin word *stringere*, meaning to bind tightly. Other sources contend that the term derives from the French word *distress*, anglized to *distress*, and suggest that the prefix *dis* was eventually eliminated because of slurring, as in the case of the word *because* sometimes becoming *'cause*.

A common generalized literal description of stress is "a constraining force or influence." When applied to the human organism, this could be interpreted to mean the extent to which the body can withstand a given force to influence. In this regard, my friend, the late Hans Selye, who was generally know as the "father of stress," described it as the "nonspecific response of the body to any demand made upon it."[1] This means that stress involves a mobilization of the body's resources in response to some stimulus (stressor). These responses can include various physical and chemical changes in the organism. This description of stress could be extended by saying that it involves demands that tax or exceed the resources of the human organism. (Selye's concept of stress will be explained in more detail later in the chapter.) This means that stress not only involves these bodily changes but that it also involves wear and tear, brought about by these responses, on the organism.

In essence, stress can be considered as any factor, acting internally or externally, that makes it difficult to adapt and that induces increased effort on the part of the individual to maintain a state of equilibrium between himself or herself and the external environment. It should be understood that stress is the *state* that one is in, and this should not be confused with any agent that produces such a state. Such agents are referred to as stressors.

## THEORIES OF STRESS

Although it is not the intent to get into a highly technical discourse on the complex and complicated aspects of stress, there are still certain basic understandings that need to be taken into account, and this requires the use of certain technical terms. For this reason it appears appropriate to proved an "on-the spot" glossary of terms used in the discussion to follow.

ACTH — (AdrenoCortico Tropic Hormone) secreted by the pituitary gland. It influences the function of the adrenals and other glands in the body.
Adrenalin — (A hormone secreted by the medulla of the adrenal glands.
Adrenals — (Two glands in upper posterior part of the abdomen that produce and secrete hormones. They have two parts, the outer layer, called the *cortex* and the inner core called the *medulla*.

---

[1] Selye, Hans, *Stress Without Distress*, New York, New American Library, 1975, p. 17.

Corticoids — Hormones produced by the adrenal cortex, an example of which is *cortisone.*
Endocrine — Glands that secrete their hormones into the blood stream.
Hormone — A chemical produced by a gland, secreted into the blood stream, and influencing the function of cells or organs.
Hypothalamus — The primary activator of the autonomic nervous system, it plays a central role in translating neurological stimuli into endocrine processes during stress reactions.
Pituitary — An endocrine gland located at the base of the brain about the size of a pea. It secretes important hormones, on of which is the ACTH hormone.

Although there are various theories of stress, one of the better known ones and one to which others are anchored, is that of the previously-mentioned Hans Selye. As mentioned, Selye's description of stress is the "non-specific response of the body to any demand made upon it." The physiological processes and the reactions involved in Selye's stress model is known as the *General Adaptation Syndrome* and consists of three stages of *alarm reaction, resistance stage* an the *exhaustion stage.*

In the first stage (alarm reaction), the body reacts to the stressor and causes the hypothalamus to produce a biochemical "messenger" which in turn cause the pituitary gland to secrete ACTH into the blood. This hormone then causes the adrenal gland to discharge adrenalin and other corticoids. This causes shrinkage of the thymus with an influence on heart rate, blood pressure, and the like. It is during the alarm stage that the resistance systems of the body are reduced.

In the second stage, *resistance* develops if the stressor is not too pronounced. Body adaptation develops to fight back the stress or possibly avoid it, and the body begins to repair damage, if any.

The third state of *exhaustion* occurs if there is a long-continued exposure to the same stressor. The ability of adaptation is eventually exhausted and the signs of the first stage (alarm reaction) reappear. Selye contended that our adaptation resources are limited, and, when they become irreversible, the result is death.

As mentioned previously, Selye's stress model, which places emphasis upon "nonspecific" responses, has been widely accepted. However, the nonspecific nature of stress has been questioned by some. This means that *psychological* stressors activate other endocrine systems beside those activated by *physiological* stressors such as cold, electric shock, and the like.

As in the case of all research, the search for truth will continue and more and more precise and sophisticated procedures will emerge in the scientific study of stress. Current theories will be more critically appraised and evaluated, and other theories will continue to be advanced. In the meantime, there is abundant evidence to support the notion that stress in modern society is a most serious threat to the well being of man if not controlled, and of course the most important factor in such control is man himself.

## REACTIONS TO STRESS

There are various ways in which reactions to stress can be classified, and, in any kind of classification, there will be some degree of unavoidable overlapping. For purposes here I arbitrarily suggest two broad classifications of *physiological* and *behavioral*.

### Physiological Reactions

Although all individuals do not always react in the same way physiologically as far as stress is concerned, the following generalized list suggests some of the more or less standard body reactions.

1. Rapid beating of the heart, which has sometimes been described as "pounding of the heart." Athletic directors and coaches experience this reaction at one time or another as a result of game excitement.
2. Perspiration, which is mostly of the palms of the hands, although there may be profuse sweating in some individuals at various other parts of the body. (Many athletic directors and coaches "sweat it out" when the game plan is not being executed properly.)
3. The blood pressure rises, which may be referred to as a hidden reaction because the individual is unlikely to be aware of it.

4. The pupils of the eyes may dilate, and, again, the individual will not necessarily be aware of it.
5. The stomach seems to "knot up," and we tend to refer to this as "feeling a lump in the pit of the stomach." This, of course, can have a negative influence on digestion.
6. Sometimes individuals experience difficulty in swallowing, which is often characterized as a "lump in the throat."
7. There may be a "tight" feeling in the chest and when the stressful condition is relieved, one may refer to it as "getting a load off my chest."

What these various bodily reactions mean is that the organism is gearing up for a response to a stressor. This phenomenon is called the *fight or flight* response and was first described as an *emergency* by Walther B. Cannon[2], the famous Harvard University Professor of Physiology, a good many years ago. The fight or flight response prepares us for action in the same way that it did for prehistoric man when he was confronted with an enemy. His responses were decided on the basis of the particular situation, such as fighting an opponent for food or fleeing from an animal that provided him with an overmatched situation. In modern times, with all the potentially stressful conditions that provide a flight or fight response, modern man uses these same physiological responses to face up to these kinds of situations. However, today, we generally do not need to fight physically (although we might feel like it sometimes), or run from wild animals, but out bodies still react with the same fight or flight response. Physiologists point out that we still need this means of self-preservation occasionally, but not in response to the emotional traumas and anxieties of modern living.

---

[2] Cannon, Walter B. *The Wisdom of the Body,* New York, W. W. Norton and Company, Inc., 1932.

## Behavioral Reactions

In discussing behavioral reactions, it should be mentioned again that various degrees of overlapping may occur between these reactions and physiological reactions. Although behavioral reactions are, for the most part, physiologically oriented, they are likely to involve more overt manifestations than are provoked by the physiological reactions. For purposes of this discussion I consider *behavior* to mean anything that one does as a result of some sort of stimulation.

A person under stress will function with a behavior that is different from ordinary behavior. These behaviors can arbitrarily be subclassified as (1) *counter* behavior (sometimes referred to as defensive behavior), (2) *dysfunctional* behavior, and (3) overt behavior (sometimes referred to as expressive behavior).

In *counter* behavior, a person will sometimes take action that is intended to counteract the stressful condition. An example is an individual taking a defensive position; that is, a person practicing an "on-the-spot" relaxation technique, but at the same time, being unaware of it. He or she may take a deep breath and silently count to ten before taking action, if any. We sometimes witness this reaction when a coach is not satisfied with an official's call. A favorite comment by media analysts when this occurs is: "Coach So and So is livid."

Dysfunctional behavior means that a person will react in a manner that demonstrates impaired or abnormal functioning, which results in a lower level of skill performance than he or she is ordinarily capable of accomplishing. There may be a change in the normal speech patterns, and there may be a temporary loss of memory. Many of us have experienced this while we attempt to get back on the original train of thought. Some football coaches have reported to me that, much to their chagrin this has happened during halftime because of a particularly stressful first half.

*Overt* behavior involves such reactions as distorted facial expressions (e.g., tics and twitches and biting the lip). There appears to be a need for a person to move about, and thus, pacing around is characteristic of this condition. Overt behavior in the form of activity can be highly effective in reducing threat and distress.

A point of interest here is that the chair-bashing and foot-stomping basketball coach is relieving himself of stress although such antics may be unacceptable to the athletic director and some fans.

## DESIRABLE AND UNDESIRABLE STRESS

The classic comment by Selye that stress is the spice of life sums up the idea that stress can be desirable as well as devastating. He went on to say that the only way one could avoid stress would be never to do anything and that certain kinds of activities have a beneficial influence in keeping the stress mechanism in good shape.

Certainly, the human organism needs to be taxed in order to function well, and it is a well-known physiological fact that muscles will soon atrophy if not subjected to sufficient use. Athletes express a desirable aspect of stress when they refer to "getting up" for a game, and feeling the "juices flowing."

At one time or another every athletic director has experienced "butterflies in the stomach" when faced with a particularly challenging situation. Thus, it is important that we understand that stress is a perfectly normal human state and that the organism is under various degrees of stress in those conditions which are related to happiness as well as those concerned with sadness.

In the literature, undesirable stress may be referred to as *distress*. It is interesting to note that Selye referred to the pleasant or healthy kind of stress as "eustress," and to the unpleasant or unhealthy kind as "distress."

I have mentioned some of the desirable features of stress, but like any factor involving the human organism, most anything excess is not good for it. Of course, this holds true for abnormal amounts of stress. When stress becomes prolonged and unrelenting, and thus, chronic, it can result in very serious health problems.

Although both "good" stress and "bad" stress reactions place specific demands for resources on the body, does it mean that good stress is "safe" and bad stress "dangerous?" Several years ago two prominent psychologists, Israel Posner and Lewis Leitner[3] made some interesting suggestions in this regard.

---

[3] Posner, Israel and Leitner, Lewis A. Eustress vs. distress: Determination by predictability and controllability of stressors, *STRESS, The Official Journal of the International Institute of Stress and Its Affiliates*, 2, Summer 1981.

They believed that two psychological variables, *predictability* and *controllability* play an important role.

It can be reasoned that *predictable* pain and discomfort is less stressful because under this condition a person is said to be capable of learning when it is safe to "lower his guard" and relax. Since periods of impending pain are signaled, the person can safely relax at times when the warning signal is absent. These periods of psychological safety seem to insulate individuals from harmful effects of stress. Obviously, persons receiving unsignalled pain have no way of knowing when it is safe to relax and thus have no way of knowing when it is safe to relax and thus are more likely to develop serious health problems as a result of the chronic psychological stress. (Certainly, a coach or athletic director should be able to predict when he or she is going into a crucial athletic contest that there will be many stressful situations involved with it.)

The second psychological variable, *controllability* of environmental stressors which is already related to coping behavior, also plays a major role in determining stress effects. The ability to control painful events may insulate individuals from experiencing damaging stress effects. However, such coping behavior is beneficial only if a person is given feedback which informs him or her that the coping response was successful in avoiding an impending stressor. Without the feedback of success, active coping behavior, as such, may increase stress effects since it calls upon the energy reserves of the body and leaves it in a state of chronic stress.

The research on predictability and controllability of stressful events may help answer why it is that people who seek out stressful and challenging activities do not appear to develop stress illnesses from this form of stress. In contrast, when essentially similar body reactivity is produced by "bad" stress, then stress-related illnesses can be the result. Perhaps "good" stress does not produce illness because typically the events associates with it are planned in advance (they are predictable) or otherwise scheduled or integrated (they are controlled) into the individual's life. However, even activities which are generally considered to be pleasant and exciting (good stress) can produce illness if the individual is not forewarned or has little control over the events. And unpleasant events (bad stress) may result in stress-related illness, because they generally come without warning and cannot be controlled.

# CAUSES OF STRESS AMONG SECONDARY SCHOOL ATHLETIC DIRECTORS

There are general causes of stress inherent in certain life events and the hassles of daily living. However, it is clear that there are specific causes of stress that are peculiar to certain populations – in this case, secondary school athletic directors. As mentioned at the outset of this chapter I asked the athletic directors in my survey to identify stress-inducing factors that they encountered on the job. In this regard, my findings were arbitrarily classified as follows: (1) outside influences, (2) personnel, (3) internal affairs, (4) scheduling, (5) time, and (6) student athletes.

## Outside Influences

By far the most stress-inducing factor concerned with outside influences was that of *parents*. In fact, it may be recalled that elsewhere in the book I commented that athletic directors have to deal with over zealous parents who have the mistaken notion that their son or daughter is a potential All-American or World Record Holder. Following are just a few of the ways that athletic directors expressed these feelings about this factor.

- Dealing with disgruntled parents
- Parent confrontation (cuts, playing time, coaching decisions)
- Parent problems and pressures
- Listening to unrealistic parents
- Angry parents
- Parents thinking they know everything
- Parents wanting to coach
- Intrusive parents
- Parents who expect special treatment for their child

Other outside influences that were stressful were stated as follows:

- Crowd control
- Booster clubs

- Media
- Pressure of post season success

## Personnel

Anyone who has a *boss type* job must deal with any number of different types of personalities, and athletic directors are no exception. Following are some of the typical types of stressors caused by personnel.

- Filling coaching vacancies
- Coaches not following school policy
- Coaches who do not support athletic policy
- Getting coaches to turn in paper work
- Evaluating poor coaches
- Poor work ethic of staff
- Officials not showing up
- Staff morale

## Internal Affairs

There are many different kinds of internal affairs that can be stressful for athletic directors and many of them were stressed by the following:

- Lack of facilities
- Financial and budget woes
- Paper work
- Lack of administrative support
- Administrative interference
- Arranging transportation
- Unreasonable expectations of administrators
- Liability for safety
- Doing other people's job
- Other administrators who don't care about athletics

## Scheduling

- Scheduling facilities for inclement weather
- Too many sports for one person to schedule
- Scheduling use of facilities
- Filling the schedule for all sports
- Weather interruptions
- Schedule conflicts

## Time

The time factor is one that has stressful effects for most administrators, athletic directors included. Following are typical time stressors.

- Lack of time
- Time on the road
- Only one of me; can't do everything
- Number of required working hours; 60-70 per week
- Never enough time
- Time commitment and expectations
- Too much night work

## Student Athletes

At the college level the greatest stressor for coaches and athletic directors are the student athletes. This is not quite so pronounced at the secondary school level; nevertheless, there are a variety of stress-inducing factors in this category. Athletic directors expressed some of them as follows:

- Discipline of athletes
- Eligibility problems
- Students violating athletic code (drugs, alcohol, tobacco)
- Training rule violations

There is no question that secondary school athletic directors face numerous problems and many of them are stress inducing. However, there are valid ways to deal with stress and this is the subject of the following discussion.

## COPING WITH STRESS

To cope means to deal with and attempt to overcome problems and difficulties. Generally speaking stress coping procedures can be divided into the two broad categories of coping *behaviors* and coping *techniques*.

### Coping Behaviors

As mentioned before, for purposes here I will consider *behavior* as anything that the human organism does as a result of some sort of stimulus. The coping behaviors that I am recommending are in the form of what I call the *Humphrey Principles of Living*. Obviously, there are no resolute standard behaviors that are guaranteed to relieve a person entirely from undesirable stress. There are, however, certain general principles in the form of behaviors that may be applied as guidelines to help alleviate stressful conditions. Thus the *Humphrey Principles of Living* should be considered as guidelines, but not necessarily in any particular order of importance. Moreover, it should be recognized that each principle is not a separate entity unto itself. This means that all of the principles are in some way interrelated and interdependent upon each other.

***Principle:*** *Personal health practices should be carefully observed.*
*Comment:* This is an easy principle to accept, but sometimes it is difficult to implement. No one is against good health, but not everyone abides by those practices that can help maintain a suitable level of health. Athletic directors with imposing schedules may be prone to neglect the basic requirements that are essential for the human organism to reach an acceptable functional level. Disregard for such important needs as a proper diet, adequate rest and sleep, sufficient physical activity, and balancing work with play can reduce the ability to deal with the stressful conditions sometimes inherent in the job.

***Principle****: Learn to recognize your own accomplishments.*

*Comment:* One must learn to recognize his or he own accomplishments and praise oneself for them, especially if such praise is not offered by others. This is generally known as "stroking," or "patting one's self on the back." In practicing this procedure one can develop positive attitudes and/or belief systems about one's accomplishments and thus reduce stress.

***Principle:*** *Learn to take one thing at a time.*

*Comment:* This is concerned with time budgeting and procrastination, and I have already mentioned the "time" factor as being stress inducing for some athletic directors. There is a need to sort out those tasks in order of importance and attack them one at a time. Proper budgeting of time can help alleviate procrastination, which in itself can be a stress-inducing factor.

***Principle:*** *Learn to take things less seriously.*

*Comment:* This should not be interpreted to mean that one's job should not be taken seriously. It does mean that there can be a fine line between what we sometimes deem to be serious but may not be so. Sometimes when people look back at a particular event, they may wonder how they could have become so concerned about it.

***Principle:*** *Do things for others.*

*Comment:* People can sometimes take their mind off their own stressful conditions by offering to do something for other persons. When individuals are helpful to others in attempting to relieve them from stress, they in turn will tend to be relieved of stress themselves. Research shows that those persons who volunteer to help others often get as much, if not more, benefit from this practice as those they volunteer to help.

***Principle:*** *Talk things over with others.*

*Comment:* People sometimes tend to keep things to themselves, and as a consequence, they may not be aware that others might be disturbed by the same stress-inducing factors. Sometimes discussing something with a fellow worker can help one see things in a much different light.

## Coping Techniques

There are a number of useful stress coping techniques, and most of them are designed to induce the *relaxation response*. This term was introduced several years ago by Dr. Herbert Benson.[4] This involves a number of bodily changes that occur in the organism when one experiences deep muscle relaxation. There is a response against "overstress" that brings on these bodily changes and brings the body back into a healthier balance. Thus the purpose of any kind of relaxation techniques should be to *induce* the relaxation response.

As previously mentioned, there are various forms of relaxation that can induce the relaxation response. The one that I have decided to focus upon here is *progressive relaxation*. It is an effective technique, and it is a procedure which is relatively easy to learn. To begin with, I will discuss some of the general aspects of relaxation.

### *The Meaning of Relaxation*

The reality of muscle fibers is that they have a response repertoire of one. All they can do is contract and this is the response they make to the electrochemical stimulation of impulses carried via the motor nerves. *Relaxation* is the removal of this stimulation.

From the point of view of the physiologist, relaxation is sometimes considered s "zero activity," or as nearly zero as one can manage in the neuromuscular system. That is, it is a neuromuscular accomplishment that results in reduction, or possible complete absence of muscle tonus in a part of, or in the entire body. A primary value of relaxation lies in lowering brain and spinal cord activity, resulting from a reduction of nerve impulses arising in muscle spindles and other sense endings in muscles, tendons, and joint structures.

The terms *relaxation, refreshment,* and *recreation* are often confused in their meaning. Although all of these factors are important to the well-being of the human organism, they should not be used interchangeably to mean the same thing. *Refreshment* is the result of an improved blood supply to the brain for "refreshment" from central fatigue and to the muscles for the disposition of their waste products. This explains in part why mild muscular activity is good

---

[4] Benson, Herbert, *The Relaxation Response,* New York, William Morrow, 1975, p. 93.

for overcoming the fatigue of sitting quietly (seventh inning stretch) and for hastening recovery after strenuous exercise (an athlete continuing for a short distance slowly after a race).

*Recreation* may be described as the experience from which a person emerges with the feeling of being "re-created." No single activity is sure to bring this experience to all members of a group, nor is there assurance that an activity will provide recreation again for a given person because it did so the last time. These are more the marks of a psychological than a physiological experience. An important essential requirement for a recreational activity is that it completely engross the individual; that is, it must engage his or her entire undivided attention. It is really escape from disintegrating effects of distractions to the healing effect of totally integrated activity. Experiences that produce this effect may range from a hard game of tennis to the reading of a comic strip.

Some individuals consider recreation and relaxation to be one and the same thing, which is not the case. Recreation can be considered a type of mental diversion that can be helpful in relieving tension. While mental and muscular tensions are interrelated, it is the muscle that the tension state is manifested.

*Learning to Relax*

One of the first steps in learning to relax is to experience tension. That is, one should be sensitive to tensions that exist in his or her body. This can be accomplished by voluntarily contracting a given muscle group, first very strongly and then less and less. Emphasis should be placed on detecting the signal or tension as the first step in "letting go" (relaxing).

You might wish to try the traditional experiment used to demonstrate this phenomenon. Raise one arm so that the palm of the hand is facing away from your face. Now, bend the writst backward and try to point the fingers back toward your face and down toward the forearm. You should also feel some *strain* at the wrist joint. You should also feel something else in the muscle and this is tension, which is due to the muscle contracting the hand backward. Now, flop the hand forward with the fingers pointing downward and you will have accomplished a *tension-relaxation cycle.*

As in the case of any muscular skill, learning how to relax takes time and one should not expect to achieve complete satisfaction immediately. After one has identified a relaxation technique that he or she feels comfortable with, increased practice should eventually achieve satisfactory results.

*Progressive Relaxation*

The technique of progressive relaxation was developed by Dr. Edmund Jacobson many years ago. It is still the technique most often referred to in the literature and probably the one that has had the most widespread application. Dr. Jacobson found that people under stress often showed signs of increased muscle tension. The mechanism producing increased muscle tension in one part of the body quite likely caused similar responses in other areas. The question raised were that if increased muscle tension caused an exaggerated reaction to stress, would the reverse be true? And, could relaxing muscles diminish disturbing physical and possible mental responses to stress? Dr Jacobson discovered that if he was able to teach his patients to relax completely all the muscles in their arms and legs, the magnitude of their response was significantly suppressed.[5]

In this technique, the person concentrates on progressively relaxing one muscle group after another. The technique is based on the procedure of comparing the difference between tension and relaxation. That is, as previously mentioned, one senses the feeling of tension in order to get the feeling of relaxation.

It has already been said that learning to relax is a skill that you can develop in applying the principles of progressive relaxation. One of the first steps is to be able to identify the various muscle groups and how to be able to identify the various muscle groups and how to tense them so that tension and relaxation can be experienced. However, before making suggestions on how to tense and relax the various muscle groups, there are certain preliminary measures that need to be taken into account.

1. You must understand that this procedure takes time and like anything else, the more you practice the more proficient you should become with the skills.

---

[5] Rosch, Paul J., Stress and muscle tension, *Health and Stress, The Newsletter of the American Institute of Stress*, No. 7, 1997, p.2.

2. Progressive relaxation is not the kind of thing to be done spontaneously, and you should be prepared to spend from 20 to 30 minutes daily in tensing-relaxing activities.
3. The particular time of day is important and this is pretty much an individual matter. Some recommendations suggest that progressive relaxation be practiced daily, sometimes during the day and again in the evening before retiring. For many people this would be difficult unless one time period was set aside before going to the job in the morning. This might be a good possibility and might help a person to start the day relaxed.
4. It is important to find a suitable place to practice the tensing-relaxing activities. Again, this is an individual matter with some preferring a bed or couch and others a comfortable chair.
5. Consideration should be given to the amount of time a given muscle is tensed. You should be sure that you are able to feel the difference between tension and relaxation. This means that tension should be maintained for about four to not more than eight seconds.
6. Breathing is an important concomitant in tensing and relaxing muscles. To begin with, it is suggested that three or more deep breaths be taken and held for five seconds or less. This will tend to make for better rhythm in breathing. Controlled breathing makes it easier to relax and it is most effective when it is done deeply and slowly. It is ordinarily recommended that one should inhale deeply and exhale slowly when "letting go."

**How to Tense and Relax Various Muscles**

Muscle groups may be identified in different ways. The classification given her consists of four different groups: (1) muscles of the head, face, tongue, and neck, (2) muscles of the trunk, (3) muscles of the upper extremities, and (4) muscles of the lower extremities.

*Muscles of the Head, Face, Tongue, and Neck*

There are two chief muscles of the head, the one covering the back of the head and the one covering the front of the skull. There are about 30 muscles of the face including muscles of the orbit and eyelids, mastication, lips, tongue, and neck. Muscles of this group may be tensed and relaxed as follows (relaxing is accomplished by "letting go" after tensing).

1. Raise your eyebrows by opening the eyes as wide as possible. You might wish to look into a mirror to see if you have formed wrinkles on the forehead.
2. Tense the muscles on either side of your nose like you were going to sneeze.
3. Dilate or flare out the nostrils.
4. Force an extended smile from "ear to ear" at the same time clenching your teeth.
5. Pull one corner of your mouth up and then the other down as in a "villainous sneer."
6. Draw your chin up close to your chest as possible.
7. Do the opposite of the above by trying to draw your head back as close to your back as possible.

*Muscles of the Trunk*

Included in this group are the muscles of the back, chest, abdomen, and pelvis. Here are some ways you can tense some of these muscles.

1. Bring your chest forward and at the same time put your shoulders back with emphasis on bringing your shoulder blades as close together as possible.
2. Try to round your shoulders and bring them up to your ears at the same time as you try to bring your neck forward.
3. Give your shoulders a shrug trying to bring them up to your ears at the same time as you try to bring your neck downward.
4. Breathe deeply and hold it momentarily and then blow out the air from your lungs rapidly.

5. Draw in your stomach so that your chest is out beyond your stomach. Exert your stomach muscles by forcing out to make it look like you are fatter in that area than you are.

*Muscles of the Upper Extremities*

This group includes the muscles of the hands, forearms, upper arms, and shoulders. A number of muscles situated in the trunk may be grouped with the muscles of the upper extremities, their function being to attach the upper limbs to the trunk and move the shoulders and arms. In view of this there is some overlapping in this and the preceding muscle group. Following are some ways to tense some of these muscles.

1. Clench the fist and then open the hand, extending the fingers as far as possible.
2. Raise one arm shoulder high and parallel to the floor. Bend at the elbow and bring the hand in toward the shoulder. Try to touch your shoulders while attempting to move the shoulder away from the hand. Flex your opposite biceps in the same manner.
3. Stretch one arm out to the side of the body and try to point the fingers backward toward the body. Do the same with the other arm.
4. Hold the arm out the same way as above but this time have the palm facing up and point the fingers inward toward the body. Do the same with the other arm.
5. Stretch one arm out to the side, clench the fist and roll the wrist around slowly. Do the same with the other arm.

*Muscles of the Lower Extremities*

This group includes muscles of the hips, things, legs, feet, and buttocks. Following are ways to tense some of these muscles.

1. Hold one leg out straight and point your toes as far forward as you can. Do the same with the other leg.
2. Do the same as above but point your toes as far backward as you can.

3. Turn each foot outward as far as you can and release. Do just the opposite by turning the foot inward as far as you can.
4. Try to draw the thigh muscles up so that you can see the form of the muscles.
5. Make your buttocks tense by pushing down if you are sitting in a chair. If you are lying down try to draw the muscles of the buttocks in close by attempting to force the cheeks together.

The above suggestions include several possibilities for tensing various muscles of the body. As you practice some of these, you will also discover other ways to tense and then let go. A word of caution might be that, in the early stages, you should be alert to the possibility of cramping of certain muscles. This can happen particularly with those muscles that are not frequently used. This means that at the beginning you should proceed carefully. It might be a good idea to keep a record of your sessions so that you can refer back to these experiences if this might be necessary. This will also help you get into each new session by reviewing your experiences in previous sessions.

In closing this final chapter, I want to again express my deep appreciation to those individuals who provided useful information and insights. Without such input, I am sure that this final volume would not have been possible.

# SUGGESTIONS FOR FURTHER READING

Boreham, C. A., Physical activity, sports participation, and risk factors in adolescents, *Medical Science in and Exercise*, p. 788-93, June 1997.

Boyd, M. P. and Zenong, Y., Cognitive-affective sources of sports enjoyment in adolescent sport participation, *Adolescence*, p. 383-95, Summer 1996.

Chapman, P., Nutrition knowledge among adolescent high school female athletes, *Adolescence*, p. 437-46, Summer 1997.

Dale, G. A., Do athletes know their strengths and weaknesses? *Strategies*, p. 22-23, May/June 1998.

Everhart, C. B. And Chellandurai, T., Gender differences in preferences for coaching as an occupation: the role of self-efficacy, valence, and perceived barriers, *Research Quarterly for Exercise and Sports*, p. 188-200, June 1998.

Ewing, B. T., High school athletes and marijuana use, *Journal of Drug Education*, p. 147-57, February 1998.

Goldberg, A. D. and Chandler, T., Sports counseling: enhancing the development of the high school student-athlete, *Journal of Counseling and Development*, p. 37-44, September/October 1995.

Holland, A. and Andre, T., Prestige ratings of high school extracurricular activities, *The High School Journal*, p. 67-72, December 1994/January 1995.

Janhunen, M. E. and Green, R. C., Injury management in high school athletes, *Coach and Athletic Director*, p. 4, December 1997.

Jones, D. C., Bridging the gap between academics and athletics, *Strategies*, p. 9-12, March/April 1998.

Lehr, C. A. and Cotton, D. J., Avoid liability potholes when transporting athletes, *Strategies*, p. 19-21, October 1995.

McEwin, C. K. and Dickinson, T. S., Placing young adolescents at risk in interscholastic sports programs, *Clearing House*, p. 217-21, March/April 1996.

Parker, P. S. M. and Read, M. H., Adolescent male athletes: body image, diet and exercise, *Adolescence*, p. 593-602, Fall 1997.

Priest, L. and Summerfield, L. M., Promoting gender equity programs, *NASSP Bulletin*, p. 52-6, December 1995.

Riley, D. B. and Arapoff, J., What food should I eat? *Coach and Athletic Director*, p. 6, March 1998.

Shuford, B. N. and Butler, D. W., Keeping the student-athlete on track, *Coach and Athletic Director*, p. 4-5, March 1998.

Smith, B. R., How to reduce the risk of sudden death in athletes, *Coach and Athletic Director,* p. 14-7, January 1998.

White, K. A., School sports events get rocked by rash of recent violent crime, *Education Week,* p. 8, May 6, 1998.

Wilson, D. J. and Sullivan, P. A., Developing leaders on athletic teams, *Strategies*, p. 18-21, January/February 1998.

# INDEX

## A

accident insurance, 40, 45, 47, 50, 71
accidents, 10, 71
activities, community, 40, 103
administration, 34, 36, 56, 60, 65, 69, 72
administrative duties, 36, 37, 54
Adrenalin, 108
advertising, 38, 43, 46, 49, 76, 79
age limitations, 74
Agility, 21
alcohol, 63, 117
All-American, 33, 115
ambulance, 38, 44, 48, 50, 71
announcements, 37, 43, 48, 50
anxiety, 6, 26
assistant principal, 42
association, athletic, 1, 63, 72, 76
Athletic Administrators Code of Ethics, 59
attendance, 74
attention deficit disorder, 5
awards, athletic, 40, 45, 47, 50, 72

## B

bad stress, 113, 114
Balance, 21
bands, 37, 45, 48, 51
Basal Metabolic Rate (BMR), 5
basketball, 1, 2, 76, 113
behavioral, 110, 112
benefit plans, 2, 66
Benefits, 78, 79
booster clubs, athletic, 40, 43, 47, 50
Boy Scouts, 99
boys, 2-6, 10, 42, 99
budget, 37, 39, 44, 46, 49, 50, 116
byes, 85, 87, 91, 96

## C

cancellation, 38, 43, 46, 49
career, v, xiii, 52
centers, community, 99
Certified Athletic Administrator, 57
Championship, 77, 87
cheerleaders, 37, 45, 48, 51, 63
Christian Associations, 99
church organizations, 99
coaching, 11, 36, 59, 105, 115, 116, 127
Code of Ethics, ix, 60, 62, 63
college, 117
competition, xiv, 4, 7-10, 40, 43, 46, 49, 63, 83, 84, 91, 94
contact sport, 11
contestants, 37, 44, 47, 49, 70, 83
contracts, 38, 43, 48, 50
controllability, 113, 114
cooperation, 8, 9, 24, 35, 55, 81, 102

curriculum, 42

## D

development, xiv, 7, 11, 13, 16, 18, 19, 22, 25, 28, 30, 31, 60, 71, 99, 127
developmental failure, 17
diaphysis, 11
digestion, 20, 111
distress, 8, 107, 112, 113
double elimination, 91, 96
driver education, 41
dropout rate, 19
drug, 63, 117

## E

educators, 2, 7, 11, 30, 58, 68, 103
elementary school, xiii, 3, 7, 11, 12, 54
eligibility requirements, 66, 74
emotional, xiii, 6, 8, 16, 18-20, 26-30, 61, 103, 111
emotionally charged, 28, 29
endurance, 3, 21, 24
energy, 4, 5, 114
equal opportunity, 2
equipment, 6, 33, 36-38, 43-51, 61, 70, 71, 81
ethics, 60
exhaustion, 109
expenditures, 37, 44, 46, 49

## F

facilities, 33, 36- 38, 44-51, 65, 70, 83, 97, 98, 116, 117
fear, 26
female, 2-6, 127
field hockey, 3
financial considerations, 80
Flexibility, 21
football, 1, 11, 39, 112
fraternal groups, 99
functions, community, 40, 99
fund-raising, 37, 45, 48, 51

## G

game supervisors, 37, 43, 46, 50
gender differences, 3, 4, 7
gender equity, 6, 128
General Adaptation Syndrome, 109
Girl Scouts, 99
girls, xiii, 2-6, 9, 10, 42, 99
goal, 14, 19
golf, 25, 76
good stress, 113, 114
grade point average, 19
groups, community, 40, 45, 48, 51, 98
guilt, 26
gymnastics, 25

## H

hate, 26
health, 15, 16, 22, 30, 34, 70, 72, 113, 114, 118
Henry, Dr. Franklin, 5
high school, 1, 19, 54, 58, 60, 62, 63, 68, 79, 127
highly competitive, 11, 12
hormonal, 4, 5
hormone, 108, 109
human rights, 60
hyperactivity, 5

## I

immaturity, 18
inclement weather, 83, 117
independence, 24
ineligibility, academic, 39, 43, 46, 49, 75
influence, 5, 26, 30, 63, 65, 100, 103, 107, 109, 113
injuries, 7, 10, 11, 39, 40, 44, 46, 47, 49, 50, 71, 72
injuries, athletic, 40, 44, 72
inspection, 37, 44, 47, 49, 70
insurance, 2, 40, 45, 47, 50, 66, 71, 72
integrated, 14, 114, 121
intellectual fitness, 30

intellectual, xiii, 5, 14, 16, 18-20, 29, 30
internal affairs, 115, 116
internet, 40, 44, 48, 51, 104, 105
interpersonal relationships, 16, 18, 25
inventory, 38, 39, 44, 46, 49, 50

## J

job analysis, xiii, 33

## L

leadership, xiv, 53-56, 59, 62, 99, 101
league, 60, 63, 85, 91
liability, iv, 71, 128
Little League elbow, 10
losers, 9, 87, 90, 91

## M

male, 4, 5, 6, 7, 41, 42, 128
maturity, 24, 28, 29
media, xiv, 2, 40, 44, 48, 51, 63, 80, 104, 106, 112
medical permits, 39, 43, 46, 49
middle school, 68
middle-aged, 22
motional disturbance, 30
municipal organizations, 99
muscles, 20-22, 113, 120, 122-126

## N

National Association for Girls and Women in Sports, 2
National Association for Sports and Physical Education (NASPE), 56
National Council of Secondary School Athletic Directors (NCSSAD), 56
National Federation of State High School Athletic Association, 1
National Interscholastic Athletic Administrators Association (NIAAA), 59, 60
negative influence, 12, 111

neuromuscular, 23, 120
non-athletes, 19

## O

objective, 14, 18, 23, 24, 28, 58
officials, athletic, 2, 66
Officials' Convention, 80
organization, 2, 36, 55, 62, 65, 66, 68, 72, 81, 101

## P

parents, 10, 11, 24, 33, 39, 43, 46, 49, 58, 59, 70, 76, 105, 106, 115
participants, xiv, 2, 11-13, 25, 27, 28, 35, 39, 41, 42, 60, 62, 66, 70-72, 83, 85
Pennsylvania Interscholastic Athletic Association (PIAA), xi, 80, 81
performance, academic, 74
permission from parents, 40, 43, 46
personality, 15, 16, 18-20, 22, 24, 26-30, 57
personnel, athletic, 72
perspiration, 21, 27
philosophy, 13-15, 19, 31, 57, 61, 74
physical education, v, xiii, 11, 23, 34, 41, 56, 68, 72
physical examination, 40, 43, 45, 47, 49, 70
physical fitness, 20, 21, 22, 24
Physical Fitness, 20, 22
physicians, 41, 45, 47, 51, 70
physiological, 3, 27, 109, 110-113, 121
play-offs, 94
point of view, 4, 15, 23, 28, 30, 120
police, 38, 44, 48, 50, 71
postponements, 38, 43, 46, 49
practice schedules, 38, 43, 46
practice, 7, 8, 15, 38-40, 43, 46, 49, 50, 61, 119, 122, 123, 126
predictability, 113, 114
preschool, 4
President's Council on Physical Fitness and Sports, 20

press releases, 40, 45, 48, 51, 80
principal, 39, 42-44, 46, 49, 54, 55, 68, 69
problem-solver, 58
program, athletic, xiv, 22, 31, 37, 40, 45, 47, 48, 51, 54, 55, 60, 65, 68-70, 75, 99-101, 103, 104, 106
progressive relaxation, 120, 122, 123
Progressive Relaxation, 122
Progressive relaxation, 123
proof of age, 40, 44, 47, 50, 74
psychological, 19, 110, 114, 121
public relations, 36, 40, 44, 47, 50, 76, 81, 97, 101-106
public safety departments, 38, 44, 48, 50
Public Schools Athletic League, 7
public schools, 36, 54, 101
purpose, 7, 14, 15, 19, 26, 35, 53, 76, 91, 96, 98, 103, 120

# R

recreation, 2, 56, 98, 99, 101, 120, 121
relaxation, 112, 120-123
relaxing, 121-124
rescheduling, 38, 43, 46, 49
resistance, 109
resources, community, 40, 98, 100
retardation, 17, 18
rivalry, 9
round robin, 91, 94, 95, 96
running, 3, 21

# S

safety, 37, 38, 44, 47-50, 70, 71, 114, 116
scheduling, 83, 115
school officials, 35, 54, 97, 98, 99
school system, 39, 44, 46, 50, 54, 55, 66, 71, 74, 101
school year, 44, 46, 50, 76
score, 38, 44, 48, 51, 74, 91
secondary school, xi, xiii, xiv, 7, 19, 33, 34, 39, 40-42, 52, 57, 59, 68, 69, 76, 115, 117, 118
self-esteem, 19

sex, 2, 5
single elimination, 83-85, 87, 91, 94, 96
soccer, 10
social, xiii, 16, 18-20, 23-25, 27, 30, 100
spectators, 27, 28, 37, 44, 47, 49, 63, 70
Speed, 21
speed, 3, 5, 9
Sponsorship, 77, 78, 79
sponsorship, corporate, 76, 81
sport season, 39, 44, 46, 50
sportsmanship, 60, 63
staff meetings, 37, 45, 47, 51
staff, 11, 37, 42, 45, 47, 51, 60, 100-104, 116
standards, 9, 24, 52, 60, 66, 74
State Athletic Association, 71
stimulation, 112, 120
stress, xiv, 6-8, 27, 42, 107-110, 112-115, 117-120, 122
stressors, 7, 107, 108, 110, 113, 114, 116, 117
substance abuse, 40, 45, 46, 50, 72
superintendent, 39, 43, 44, 46, 49, 54, 55, 58, 68, 72, 75, 101
supervision, 8, 12, 54, 71
swimming, 21, 25, 98

# T

teenagers, 24
tennis elbow, 10
tennis, 10, 25, 121
tense, 122, 124-126
tension-relaxation cycle, 121
ticket sales, 37, 43, 48, 51, 75
tobacco, 63, 117
total personality, ix, 15-20, 30
transportation, 38, 43, 47, 49, 116

# U

unethical, 63
uniforms, 38, 45, 47, 51

## W

website, 40, 48, 51, 104
winners, 4, 9, 90, 94
women's suffrage, 7
World Record Holder, 33, 115
wrestling, 3

## Y

youth groups, 41, 45, 48, 51